HANDBOOK OF AUDIO-VISUAL AIDS AND TECHNIQUES FOR TEACHING ELEMENTARY SCHOOL SUBJECTS

by ARTHUR B. GOODWIN

Here's a giant handbook filling a long-existing and critical need. Fifteen full chapters give you new and innovative techniques for making your audio-visual aids program more meaningful and effective.

Unlike many contemporary guidebooks, which tell you only how to operate the equipment, this ultra-modern handbook brings you and your students many more benefits.

Arranged in a brand new way, this handy volume enables you to plan your lessons by subject area—not by category of audio-visual aid, thus lightening your work load immeasurably.

Many chapters deal with a single subject. They show you which audio-visual aids can best be used to improve learning of that subject, and give you hundreds of ready-to-use activities.

This invaluable guidebook will give you mammoth help in each subject area:

READING: How to use the tape recorder to teach phonetics, improve listening skills and pronunciation, associate symbols and sounds, and measure reading progress. How to use the opaque projector for eye movement training, and for teaching visual discrimination. How to use the overhead projector to improve vocabulary, word analysis, comprehension, and recall interpretation. How to use motion pictures, filmstrips and slides to aid in individualized and remedial programs, to show story development, graphically illustrate characters, and improve story-telling techniques.

You'll also get pointers on using the bulletin board and flannel board to create interest, dramatize stories, show plot development, foster oral and written expression, and teach word sequence in sentences.

MATHEMATICS: How you can use the tape recorder as a drillmaster, reviewer, or reinforcer, to boost proficiency in mental computation and problem solving. How to use

HANDBOOK OF
AUDIO-VISUAL AIDS AND
TECHNIQUES FOR TEACHING
ELEMENTARY SCHOOL
SUBJECTS

HANDBOOK OF
AUDIO-VISUAL AIDS AND
TECHNIQUES FOR TEACHING
ELEMENTARY SCHOOL
SUBJECTS

Arthur B. Goodwin

Parker Publishing

Company, Inc.

West Nyack, N.Y.

PRINTED IN THE UNITED STATES OF AMERICA

13-374090-0   B & P

To My Wife, Dorothy
and
To Kenneth
and Kathleen

ACKNOWLEDGMENTS

As is the case with most authors, this book would not have seen the light of day without the cooperation and encouragement of my family. I am deeply indebted to the learning specialists in the audio-visual field, especially Dr. Louis Forsdale of Teachers College, Columbia University. I am very grateful to the countless number of teachers whose practical suggestions and information provided the main guidelines for this narrative. A deep bow of gratitude goes to Colonel Leslie B. Carpenter and Mr. Carl E. Goodwin for help in proofreading the manuscript and for constructive criticism. I am also grateful to the Huntington Public Library, Long Island, New York, for providing me with numerous professional books and magazines which were so helpful in the research phase in evolving this book. I acknowledge heartily the cooperation of four of my co-workers at the Pulaski Road School in Northport: Mrs. Frances Trepel, Mrs. Evelyn Benjamin, Miss Margaret Danes and Mr. Henry Jennings for their assistance in the initial stages of developing this manuscript. A final thanks goes to each of the manufacturers, educational organizations, school systems, individuals and educators for allowing me to use their photographs to illustrate this book.

A WORD FROM THE AUTHOR
ABOUT THIS BOOK

Today's elementary classroom teacher is often confronted with a multitude of audio-visual materials, media and techniques in his daily educational environment. This impressive array must at times seem like a technical and instructional labyrinth to most teachers. In addition, the everyday role of the classroom instructor has steadily become more demanding with the pressures of increasing amounts of subject matter to be mastered and taught besides still having the routine number of classroom responsibilities and non-teaching duties.

A significant question raised by teachers is, "How can we effectively apply the various implements and materials of audio-visual instruction which are available directly to our own particular grade level, subject area and classroom situation?" Of course, there are many outstanding authoritative textbooks that answer the question on the utilization of audio-visual equipment as well as numerous books concerned with various audio-visual media and their techniques. Perhaps what many classroom teachers most urgently desire is a simplified but comprehensive handbook to which they can readily refer for sources of practical audio-visual ideas and suggestions that can be put into immediate practice.

This handbook was written by an elementary classroom teacher with seventeen years experience in grades three to six, further supplemented by his ten years experience as an audio-visual building coordinator.

Each topic was carefully researched and leading authorities in the elementary educational and audio-visual fields were consulted throughout the preparation of the manuscript. This text is intended for our country's vast audience of elementary classroom instructors, educational specialists and elementary administrators. Practicality is the dominant theme of each of the units so that technical verbiage and pronouncements of philosophy and lofty theory are avoided. The entire narrative has been put down in a straightforward, informal style of prose to make for greater readability.

This text differs from most audio-visual books on the market in that it is primarily grouped according to subject matter fields rather than the usual arrangement by classification of materials, media and methods. This departure in presentation should help the reader avoid the tiresome necessity for skipping around the book in order to find a good idea or suggestion for tomorrow's science lesson or the following day's reading lesson.

The various self-contained units deal with the most pertinent subject matter areas in the elementary curriculum. The differences between the primary and intermediate levels of instruction are allowed for in the suggestions in each commentary about applicable audio-visual materials and techniques for specific subject matter areas.

A novel feature in this handbook is that individual sections are given over to practical guidelines for effective utilization of tools and techniques of audio-visual materials by educational specialists in music, art, physical education and library science. Another phase of the handbook is concerned with ideas for educational field trips and community resources. The final chapter of the book contains recommendations to teachers on how they can keep in stride with the latest audio-visual trends and techniques as they apply to the elementary curriculum. Also included is a helpful list of innovative audio-visual ideas that can be adapted to specific areas of elementary teaching.

The last section of the book contains a directory of leading audio-visual manufacturers and a bibliography that combines a list of authoritative texts on audio-visual methods and materials.

The important thing about teaching with audio-visual materials is their effective use, not their flagrant abuse. Audio-visual materials, media and techniques should not be looked upon for gimmick or novelty values, but should serve instead mainly as stimuli to make each teacher a more creative and engrossing teaching personality. Therefore, it is hoped that the various ideas herein described will serve as a catalyst for more imaginative instruction in our nation's elementary school community.

CONTENTS

2. Teaching Reading More Effectively with Audio-Visual Aids (*Continued*)

3. Audio-Visual Techniques for Improving Written and Oral Expression (*Continued*)

3. **Audio-Visual Techniques for Improving Written and Oral Expression** (*Continued*)

HANDBOOK OF
AUDIO-VISUAL AIDS AND
TECHNIQUES FOR TEACHING
ELEMENTARY SCHOOL
SUBJECTS

1

HOW TO
GET THE MOST OUT
OF EACH
AUDIO-VISUAL DEVICE

In education we often have the tendency to put too much emphasis on terminology. The major role of audio-visual materials is to give spoken words and printed symbols meaning and life. These materials, if used intelligently, can prove to be far superior to other methods of instruction for purposes of motivation, retention of facts, and fostering positive attitudes and values. Most important, they accelerate the learning process because they help pupils master more subject matter and sharpen their learning skills in a shorter space of time. It is a fact that creative teaching is accomplished when new audio-visual techniques and materials are judiciously blended and carefully integrated into our modern elementary school curriculum. In the past generation, imaginative and flexible audio-visuals have been made more available. Today's teacher must keep pace and be well informed about the latest in audio-visual techniques so that he is challenged to become a more skillful and inventive instructor, and will, in turn, challenge his students in such a way that the classroom will become a truly fascinating and meaningful place in which to learn.

Now let us explore the distinguishing characteristics and advantages, with some reflections on the weaknesses, of certain major audio-visual devices used in our elementary schools.

AUDIO DEVICES IN INSTRUCTION

Tape Recorder

No audio device has made as much impact on the American educational scene in the past decade as the tape recorder, and, like its aural predecessor, the record player, it has become commonplace in our classrooms. What especially makes this device so valuable to teachers is its flexibility, since it can be tailored to conform to large class instructional situations or individualized and remedial forms of instruction. With thoughtful planning and a sprinkling of imagination, tape recordings may be incorporated into any curriculum area, whether it be reading, oral language, social studies, science, math or music. Audio tapes can preserve radio programs for future use and act as a vehicle for reviewing and testing. Tapes serve well in developing good listening habits and provide unrestricted opportunities for oral expression and evaluation. Furthermore, teachers will find the tape recorder ideal for supplying an aural record for guidance folders and for use in parent conferences. The tape recorder can serve as an audio means to assist teachers in reflecting and evaluating their own oral presentations and improving on them.

A development of great promise for the school tape instructional program is the current introduction of the cartridge tape. Since this is a relatively recent innovation at the school level, it is recommended that the reader follow the developments in this area in such monthly periodicals as *Educational Screen AV Guide* and *Audiovisual Instruction*. Certainly, the tape cartridge will help the teacher overcome some of the minor difficulties associated with regular tape reel threading.

Phonograph

Although small inexpensive portable record players are available in practically all classrooms, it is questionable if this older audio standby is being utilized as extensively as it should. For years, most teachers have been using this media tool as background for music appreciation, classroom singing or reading. Recently, there have been several unique developments in the technology and utilization of this media. Commercial record manufacturers are producing special record-book combinations in which the record relates the story as the child turns the pages. Two companies manufacturing this type of record are: Golden Records, a division of A. A. Records, Inc., with the "Read and Hear" series, which is available on 45 rpm records, and Walt Disney Productions with the "See the pictures, Hear the record, Read the book" series, available on 33⅓ long playing records. Another major trend is the development of records to accompany the commercial filmstrip and slide presentation for all subject areas.

Favorite and rare records have an everlasting value when transferred to tape. In this way, if the record is later lost or damaged, a copy of the recording is preserved. Since tapes of disc recordings can be readily duplicated, the original disc record can be stored and the tape played for classroom use.

It is perhaps at the primary level that records are most frequently used to present children's stories, music and poetry. At the intermediate level they are a permanent record of past events, and they allow the teacher to bring actual voices of outstanding political, scientific and social leaders into the educational environment. The top talents of professional writers and actors are available for imaginative dramatizations which can be the catalyst for motivation of numerous activities at all levels.

The type of phonograph you may select will vary, depending on the group you have and the subject you are teaching. Certainly, for the best in music reproduction, you will need a machine with high fidelity sound, but for general classroom use, a simple, inexpensive one- or two-knob record player will suffice.

Most record players sold to schools have four speeds. Some machines have pause controls so that a record may be readily stopped without jarring the stylus at any point, thus avoiding damage to the record or needle (Figure 1-1). There are also phonographs that have variable speed controls that permit the teacher to control the turntable speed above or below the usual four record speeds. Usually, phonographs have a dual stylus cartridge where one side operates at 78 rpm, and which, if flipped over, can be used for microgroove recordings. It is important that if your school is using a monaural type of equipment, one must make certain that *stereo records are not played on a monaural machine* since the records may be damaged. There is usually no problem, however, in playing a monaural record on a stereo player. Finally, a long-lasting diamond needle is preferred over the short-lived sapphire. A worn or wrong needle can raise havoc with precious recordings.

Radio

Sometimes, because of the dominance of television media, we forget that commercial and educational radio have made important strides. Commercial radio has tailored formats with greater emphasis on music, on-

Figure 1-1
Audio-Tronic Pause Control

Courtesy of Audiotronics Corporation, No. Hollywood, Calif.

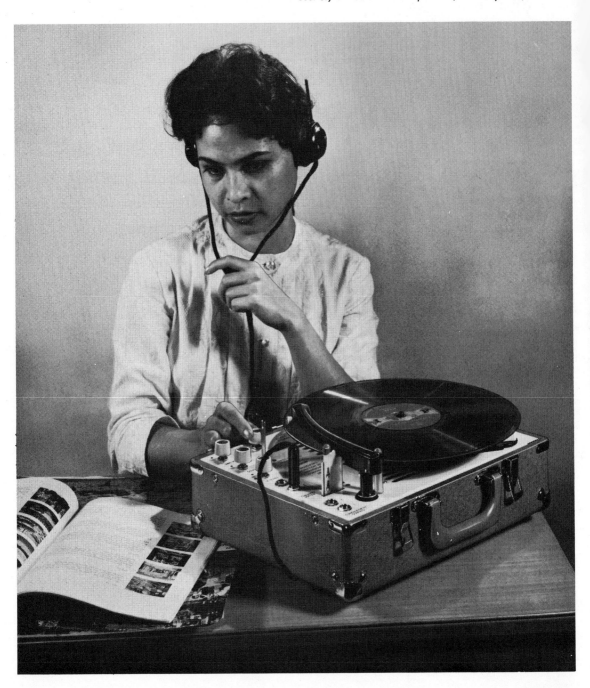

the-spot news and discussion programs. Technically, there have been greater advances with the advent of inexpensive FM receivers, and the introduction of FM stereo broadcasts and the always accessible standard AM broadcasts. Most large city school systems have available to them educational FM programming.

Radio makes all who listen aware of the importance of audio stimuli in learning and gives us an appreciation of the beauty of the voice. Radio, with the combination of its aural qualities of music, voice and sound effects, stirs within us deep emotional experiences which will magically lead us to more significant and imaginative learning.

No discussion of radio can be considered complete without mention of the tremendous potential and creative learning possibilities of educational radio. The sites of presently existing radio outlets are primarily state universities and municipalities. There are and have been some outstanding programs emitted from New York (WNYE), Newark (WBGO), Detroit (WDTR), Cleveland (WBOE) and St. Louis (KSLH). While there are some local school districts that operate their own stations, they are unfortunately in the minority. Perhaps the solution to the problem lies in cooperative ventures such as New York's Empire State FM School of the Air. This audio network, begun in 1947, now extends into the far reaches of that vast state.

The FM or AM educational radio station has a definite advantage over the strongly financed commercial station in that educational radio programs can be geared to meet specific pupil needs and interest levels in such learning areas as literature, language arts, current events, science and health, and music appreciation. A good example of this is the 1967-68 programming of New York City's educational outlet, WNYE. This station offered such diverse topics as "Tales from the Four Winds," "Listen and Write," "It's Fun to Sing," "The Negro in America," "Americans to Remember," and "Pioneers of Science."

A most informative commentary on the uses of educational radio is expounded in detail in Dr. Herbert E. Scuorzo's book, *The Practical Audio-Visual Handbook for Teachers,* published by the Parker Publishing Company, Inc. To find specific information on programming in your own locality, it is suggested that you contact your state department of education.

NON-PROJECTED MATERIALS

Textbooks

The textbook, often called the hard core of teacher preparation or the foundation of most teachers' instructional programs, has improved steadily in the degree of scholarship, research and illustrative material presented. Today, book publishers package their material in a flexible, well-organized and readable format; likewise, book manufacturers provide teachers' editions that contain not only a rich source of ideas and activities but also a listing of available audio-visual materials correlated to the printed product.

Textbooks are an extremely valuable source of information in any subject area, and they augment the teacher's instructional program. They provide each student with his own outline of the subject area being studied. Since most books are well-balanced and structured they give the pupil the continuity so vital to elementary school pupils.

The textbook should not be the sole basis of classroom instruction. Nothing can be more damaging to learning than a teacher who rigidly follows the textbook verbatim and gives meaningless assignments from the textual material. Although the vast majority of textbooks are sound educationally and visually appealing, educators who select textual materials must carefully evolve a set of standards that takes into account such criteria as the treatment of subject matter, the size and type of print, as well as the pupil's age.

Graphics, Posters, Charts and Related Materials

Perhaps the greatest value of such graphics as magazine illustrations and related visual materials is that they help provide vicarious experiences which develop pupil insight or understanding, make facts more vivid, and motivate meaningful research. Materials such as charts, graphs and diagrams help present abstract ideas or symbolism in visual form. These pictorials assist pupils in understanding the relationship of facts and statistics. They help evolve a sense of continuity in the learning process and function well as a means of summarizing or reviewing information.

In the selection of illustrations and flat pictures, we should choose materials that are large enough for pupils to see and material that is not only attractive, but accurate. The best pictures and illustrations should be incorporated in bulletin board displays. When employing any graphic for teaching purposes, we must avoid those that encompass too much visually, or charts and diagrams loaded with too much printed information or an overabundance of statistics.

Some ideal sources of flat pictures are magazines with extensive pictorial sections; namely, *Fortune, Life, Look, Holiday, House Beautiful* or *Better Homes and Gardens.* If you have difficulty securing back issues of these magazines, send out an SOS to your pupils' parents, your fellow teachers or your school P.T.A.

If you are already experienced in photography, on your next trip take a series of pictures that will be of interest to your class. Make your photos even more valuable by writing down significant comments about the circumstances under which the pictures were taken. Your notes will, at a later date, provide an interesting commentary when the pictures are shown to the class.

One of the most valuable social studies picture teaching aids is the poster. Actually, a poster is a large picture that, at a glance, conveys one or two main ideas to the viewer. For this reason, posters contain very little accompanying printed narration.

There are many free or inexpensive, splendidly produced posters that may be obtained from tourist bureaus, travel agencies, foreign embassies, United States government agencies, manufacturers and associations such as the Association of American Railroads. Bruce Miller's *Sources of Free Travel Posters and Geographic Aids* contains much useful information on securing posters and chart materials. Professionally-made posters serve as a frame of reference for the student-made production.

Maps and Globes Teachers use maps and globes as companion items for classroom instruction since they act to complement each other. There is a wide variety of maps and globes that enhance almost any subject area. Furthermore, there are many excellent types of maps which depict such areas, from population to climate or topography to history. Commercial map makers provide primary grades with maps which are simply colored, that use large lettering and contain a sensible minimum of symbols. In the upper grades, there are raised relief maps and globes for geography, celestial globes for science and astronomy, and study maps and globes that can be marked easily with a grease pencil or chalk and wiped off without much effort.

Manufacturers of maps and globes are making materials that are not only graded as math and reading materials, but are also durable and easier for both pupils and teachers to handle physically. For example, many globes come with removable mountings so that anyone can detach the globe and place it in an attractive and natural teaching position.

PROJECTED MATERIALS

Opaque Projector

The opaque projector is distinguished from other projection materials in that it is primarily used to project a pictorial image with translucent materials or surfaces of objects that are not transparent (Figure 1-2). It

Figure 1-2

Opaque Projector

Courtesy of American Optical Corporation, Buffalo, N.Y.

is an invaluable teaching aid in the elementary classroom because of its capacity to show with ease a multitude of materials such as flat pictures, photographs, student drawings, printed matter and small opaque objects without extensive preparation. It allows a high degree of pupil involvement or participation.

Mechanically, the opaque projector is large and bulky, and for this reason it should be placed on a portable projection stand. Because of the mirror reflection system, the opaque must be used in a thoroughly darkened room. Teachers utilizing older opaque projectors must exercise caution in leaving books and bulky printed matter in the machine, since there is the possibility of heat damage. Newer machines have ventilating systems with improved fans to prevent scorching of material while keeping the pages of a book from fluttering. Most opaques have a pointer or arrow which may be used in map study to single out important objects in visuals and to emphasize pertinent facts in printed materials.

Overhead Projector

The overhead projector (Figure 1-3) might appear to some teachers to be a sort of mechanical monster; yet the overhead is a very simple visual device to run. Its basic operation involves focusing a beam of light through a sheet of flat plastic, usually termed a transparency, which immediately results in a large projected image on the screen. All a teacher has to do to operate the overhead is place a transparency over a window known as the stage, flip the power switch, and focus the image by rotating an easy-to-operate knob.

This remarkable piece of audio-visual equipment first came into use in World War II for training large groups of servicemen. Contrary to overzealous advocates of this versatile media, it has not made completely obsolete the traditional chalkboard, but it does permit face-to-face instruction and can be used in a lighted room without a diffusion of the image.

There are many companies that specialize in manufacturing projectors (portable and permanent) as well as distributing commercial acetates. Manufacturers make professionally-designed transparencies on a wide range of topics which can be adapted or incorporated into any subject area. However, teachers have the option to prepare their own transparencies. No special skills are required to make your own transparencies. You simply write, with a grease marking pencil, on the plastic sheet and lay it on the projector stage. The writing can easily be removed from the transparency with a dampened soft cloth or facial tissue (Figure 1-4).

Courtesy of American Optical Corporation, Buffalo, N.Y.

Figure 1-3
Portable Overhead Projector

Teachers can prepare polished transparent copies of pictures, charts and illustrations that are transposed from magazines and books. This can be accomplished by utilizing an infrared copying machine. To master the technique of preparing transparencies, you may take an in-service audio-visual course, when offered in your school district, or read the many manuals and books on this phase of overhead projection. One excellent book for familiarizing teachers with the transparency technique, and all other aspects of the overhead projector, is Morton J. Schultz's *The Teacher and Overhead Projection,* published by Prentice-Hall.

Figure 1-4

Under teacher's guidance pupils actively conduct a lesson with overhead projector

Filmstrips, Slides and Related Materials

The silent slidefilm or filmstrip is one of the most frequently used of the projected media (Figure 1-5). Perhaps this is due to the numerous easy-to-operate filmstrip projectors. Filmstrips, which actually are a series of individual pictures, provide on small rolls, non-inflammable, 35mm motion picture film which is particularly attractive, not only because of its overall technical excellence, but also its low cost.

Since their first introduction in the 1920's, filmstrips have steadily improved in quality and variety. Color adds immeasurably to the slide-

Courtesy of Bell & Howell Company, Audio-Visual Products Division

Figure 1-5

Silent Filmstrip Projector

The Bell & Howell Autoload Filmstrip Projector (The modern filmstrip machine)

film, and there is an increasing movement toward using slidefilms synchronized with devices like the tape recorder or disc record player (Figure 1-6).

Courtesy of Dukane Corporation Audio-Visual Division, St. Charles, Ill.

Figure 1-6

Dukane A-V Matic Sound Filmstrip Projector

Slides (3½ x 4″), popular for many decades, are still being used, but in a decreasing degree, since many schools are phasing them out. These visuals have been replaced by the more adaptable, easier to prepare and procure 2 x 2″ slide transparency. Commercial producers make available a wide pictorial array of historic shrines, geographical subjects and themes of a scientific nature for educators to choose from.

Eastman Kodak Company of Rochester has published an up-to-date pamphlet listing major companies that sell slides. This brochure is entitled "Some Sources of 2 x 2″ Color Slides" and may be obtained upon written request. There are excellent slides available on such subjects as social studies and science from the following companies: General Aniline & Film Corporation of Portland, Oregon, and the Society for Visual Education, Inc. of Chicago, Illinois.

Motion Pictures

Both 8mm and 16mm motion pictures cover an extensive range of subject matter in elementary teaching. These include how-to-do-it films as well as scientific, informational, storytelling, news, recreational, industrial, entertainment and appreciation films.

In the past few decades 16mm sound motion pictures have dominated the educational scene and will probably do so in the years to come. However, the technological advances in the film field, especially with the development of easier-to-operate projectors, the advent of Kodak's Super 8 with enlarged picture, and the introduction of the single concept film by such companies as the Fairchild and Technicolor Corporations, are creating a whole new approach to learning. Most single concept films, often termed *film loops,* of one minute to five minutes in duration, are generally based on science, safety, and physical education topics. Many of the single concept films are silent, but they are excellent for note-taking

Figure 1-7

Kodak Pageant 16mm Sound Projector

Courtesy of Eastman Kodak Company

purposes and individual instruction. Companies producing film loops are presently devoting much time and research in developing a trouble-free 8mm sound film utilizing film cartridges, not needing threading or any other special technical knowledge.

The 16mm motion picture has certain distinct advantages over the 8mm with its larger screen image, longer running time, greater detail and overall professionalism (Figure 1-7). A wide selection of films is

available from educational producers and commercial film exchanges. There is also a wealth of free, sponsored films from such organizations as Modern Talking Picture Service, Inc., 1212 Avenue of the Americas, New York, N.Y. 10036 or Ford Motor Company, Motion Picture Dept., Dearborn, Michigan. The newer 16mm projectors are equipped with

Courtesy of RCA

Figure 1-8

RCA 1600 Projector with Automatic Safe-Threader

automatic threading (Figure 1-8), keeping pace with a similar development in the 8mm film media.

Television

Very few people, especially educators, would dispute the fact that television is the most fascinating means of communication man has yet devised. It transmits pictures and sound in the wink of an eye, spanning both time and space. Commercial television, with its introduction of color, is making the medium not only more aesthetically exciting, but above all else, more realistic.

There are three types of television available to teachers: commercial television programming; regular educational programming, which can be received from a distance of 45 to 70 miles; and closed-circuit television, transmitted over a coaxial cable, its viewing area restricted only by the length of the cable. For educational purposes, the closed-circuit system is devoid of licensing problems from the Federal Communications Commission and can be operated by school personnel any time and in any way they wish.

The introduction of the video tape recorder to the television media allows for a greater degree of flexibility in scheduling, since any program can be taped, stored and shown at the opportune time.

Commercial television, with its massive resources, probably produces most of the truly outstanding enrichment programs, but educational television is at its best when a master teacher, in a specific subject area, is teaching with appropriate audio-visuals. The classroom teacher should look upon the television teacher as a partner or team-teaching aid, each in his own way providing pertinent information, creating activities, stimulating the imagination, and contributing in a positive manner to children's experiences.

Although commercial television has been attacked as a vast wasteland wallowing in mediocrity, a fine choice of educational programs for classroom instruction is available—if the teacher will take the time to check through a good television guide—e.g., Walt Disney's "Wonderful World of Color" has frequently presented programs with themes on natural science and geographical or historical interest. Some sources of pure educational television programming are the state and local P.T.A. offices, the U.S. Office of Education (Radio and Television Section), the National Association of Educational Broadcasters, your home state department of education, nearby colleges and universities, and county or district audio-visual instructional materials centers.

DISPLAY MATERIALS

Bulletin Board and Flannel Board

Bulletin boards, one of the oldest visuals, along with the flannel and felt boards, models, dioramas and exhibits are the ideal vehicles for display for all to view and from which all pupils will learn. They have been an integral part of the everyday instructional program of the past, and they still have the same impact in today's scheme of education. The creative teacher will evolve bulletin board presentations that allow pupil participation, foster a stimulating classroom environment, present a concept skillfully and systematically, and extend and enhance learning.

The flannel board is basically a piece of wool, cotton, flannel or felt, stretched tightly over a firm surface such as plywood or Masonite. While commercially-produced cutout material is available, teachers may make their own adhering visual cutouts, from cards and pictures, by gluing the pictures selected to pieces of felt and flannel so that they will adhere to the flannel board. The flannel board is an ideal media for showing steps in a process to visualize number concepts, story sequences and to demonstrate movements and arrangements. Because of the elements of simplicity and pupil participation, it is a particularly attractive device for primary pupils.

Chalkboard

The blackboard, no longer manufactured in black, is now passé and has been replaced by the *chalkboard*. Although the chalkboard is one of the easiest and fastest methods of visualizing, it requires the best of a teacher's skills and techniques to develop chalkboard presentations that will hold a pupil's interest. This flexible instructional device, which can be erased quickly so that up-to-date material can be substituted, is an excellent way to list principles, concepts and thoughts and to involve pupils instantaneously in the learning process.

Models and Dioramas

Both models and dioramas, whether of the commercial or homemade variety, are surefire display attractions in the classroom because they give the illusion of authenticity. Working models, in particular, allow pupils to examine things so they may see how they are constructed and how they function.

PERSONALIZED LEARNING EXPERIENCES

Dramatizations and Field Trips

Both dramatizations and field trips are classified as personalized experiences because active student participation is the key ingredient of both learning media. (Chapter 13 of the text will be entirely devoted to a comprehensive study of field trips with emphasis on guidelines for such visitations.) Dramatic expression is one of man's oldest forms of communication between the participants. It is the person-to-person medium which substitutes and reconstructs actual experiences and encourages pupils to use their imagination and express their feelings. Important too is its value in promoting group cooperation, and instilling confidence and poise in pupils.

The Newer Media

Some of the newer and innovative audio-visual materials can be cataloged under the title of individualized experiences such as teaching machines, programmed learning and computer assisted teaching systems. These newer aids will be discussed, and their exciting promise for the future explained in the concluding chapter of the text.

2

TEACHING READING
MORE EFFECTIVELY
WITH
AUDIO-VISUAL AIDS

The tremendous instructional potential of audio-visual materials must be fully realized in today's reading program. Tape recordings, for example, are an ideal aural means for stimulating interest in reading because of their direct appeal to a pupil's imagination and creative abilities. The tape recorder preserves the best in radio-record story dramatizations as well as being an appropriate channel for pupil self-expression. The tape recorder functions as one of the most attractive means of teaching phonetics.

The opaque projector is a basic tool in reading because of its capacity to magnify printed materials, permitting pupils to concentrate more fully on the text. The overhead projector is considered an effective implement for drawing out skills in visual discrimination and comprehension.

Filmstrips and slides are excellent devices for teaching sequential concepts, besides being highly imaginative aids for providing vicarious visual experience so vital in reading. An uncaptioned filmstrip can serve to teach sequential understanding, since pupils try to develop their own version of the story line. One series intended for primary level and entitled "Picture Stories for Reading Readiness Series, 1 and 2" (produced by Jam Handy Organization, 2821 E. Grand Boulevard, Detroit, Michigan 48211), has been devised in such a way that it is based on experiences common to primary age pupils and designed to meet their interest level.

Eye Gate House, Inc., 146-01 Archer Avenue, Jamaica, N.Y. 11435, introduced the "Read & Tell" color series which is highly suitable for teaching sequential understandings. Each filmstrip in the series relates an appealing children's story with a combined picture and caption. The second half of each filmstrip cleverly repeats the pictures without captions, thus permitting pupils to write the stories in their own words and providing them with experience in observation and recall.

Motion pictures can exert a strong influence in stimulating the powers of reflective thinking and reasoning. In addition, successful motion pictures require a high degree of organizational skill, a technique which is most desirable in the mastery of reading.

The utilization of textual and related materials is not to be treated as an end in itself. Actually, it should serve as a stepping stone to a wide range of exercises in vocabulary building, interpretation and comprehension, as well as initiating creative experiences in oral and written language.

Activities-describing bulletin boards should be primarily promotional and motivational in nature, with a great deal of emphasis on pupil involvement. The same basic ingredient of student participation is of the utmost importance in using the flannel board, the ideal vehicle for story dramatization in grades K to 3.

THE TAPE RECORDER

The tape recorder is of inestimable value for preparing introductions to new reading units and themes as well as acquainting the reader with authors and their books. At the primary level it is the proper instrument for imaginative reading readiness activities. In the upper grades, in addition to becoming increasingly important as a device to assist the teacher in evaluating a pupil's progress, the tape recorder enables pupils to have a better grasp of phonetics and improves listening skills.

Audio Background for Reading Readiness

Children at the primary level need to readily associate sound in their environment with the printed symbols representing these sounds. Teachers could record such familiar sounds in a child's environment as dishes rattling in the sink, birds chirping, dogs barking, the door bell ringing, an automobile starting or airplanes flying overhead. These familiar sounds are ideal background for reading readiness.

Phonetics Tapes for Teaching

Commercial or teacher-created phonic tapes can make drill on this phase of reading more palatable. Exercises in word analysis, consonant blends, synonyms, homonyms, antonyms and diphthongs, may be derived from old reading texts and workbooks.

Tapes for Motivation

Tape recordings from records, radio broadcasts, and teacher-pupil dramatizations based on classic children's stories, may be employed to motivate the reading of other books with similar themes; for example, a recording of Robert Louis Stevenson's *Treasure Island* could lead to reading books based on pirate adventures and related legends.

Supplementary Story Tapes

Story tapes, when accompanied with dittoed copies of the same story, will allow the pupil to listen and read the story simultaneously. At the same time the teacher can circulate around the classroom to afford students individual help. Teacher-directed exercises, based on the story's content, as well as a list of recommended class activities, may also be distributed.

Talking Story Book Kits

One interesting reading technique which has proved highly successful in the Northport, New York, and New York City schools is the Talking Story Book plan. The basic idea is to set up a media kit that contains several copies of a famous children's story, accompanied by the teacher's tape recorded narration of the same story. Supplementary books and drawings, disc recordings, filmstrips, slides and other enrichment material may also be included in attractive portfolios (Figure 2-1).

Reading Evaluation Tapes

Tapes made of pupils during reading lessons are an excellent means of measuring the reading progress of pupils. Individual students could read pre-determined passages of material appropriate to their levels. Besides obvious attention being given to oral expression and word analysis skills, some emphasis can be devoted to comprehension in the tapings. Tapes of this nature are ideal for teacher analysis, pupil self-evaluation and invaluable in parent conferences. Inventory tapes should be made approximately three times a year. Pertinent information such as recording date, pupil's name and the identity of the reading selection should be listed.

Figure 2-1
Talking Story Book

Music to Read By

Music hath charms, so why not play taped soft mood music during free reading or library periods? Appropriate music can put the reader in the proper frame of mind for reading new stories and for creative writing exercises.

PRIMARY ACTIVITIES

Mental Imagery   Listen to a taped dramatization of a classic children's story. Ask pupils to list descriptive words and phrases used in the story. These words and phrases are conducive to exercises in sentence construction and creative poetry. The teacher should offer aid to any pupil having difficulty in recording spelling words. A further extension of this activity is to encourage pupils to make sketches depicting characters or events in the dramatization.

Choral Reading of Poetry   Teachers should frequently tape choral reading of passages of poetry similar to "The Owl and the Pussy-Cat" and the English carol "I Saw Three Ships A-Sailing." This is a tape recording activity well suited for primary levels and equally adaptable to sophisticated students in the upper grades.

"Do Tell the Ending"   Tape an interesting, but unfamiliar story, for class presentation, then stop the tape before the story reaches its climax. Have committees of pupils tape their version of how the story ends. Encourage groups to construct various endings, some sad, some happy, some surprised and perhaps some with disappointing endings. In the final phase of this activity, the teacher, of course, divulges the actual ending.

INTERMEDIATE ACTIVITIES

Oral Expression   The teacher tapes a story from a book, magazine or newspaper, and uses different tones of voice to denote various emotions. After the tape is played, students are asked to re-tell a portion of the story imitating expressions and inflections.

Taped Book Reviews   Let the class present the taped reports in the format of a movie or television preview. Allow a three- to five-minute time period for each pupil to preview his book. Add an element of suspense by not revealing the title until the conclusion of the oral review.

Succinct Digest   Tape a series of short, simple, but unfamiliar stories. After playing the tape, ask the class to make up titles and re-tell the plot in one or two sentences.

Taped Biographies The teacher prepares a narrative tape on an author's background, based on his autobiography, biography or other reference material. Before playing the tape, the teacher helps familiarize the class with some of the author's literary works. Have pupils use a wall map to show the locations of places mentioned in the author's taped biography.

THE OPAQUE PROJECTOR

The opaque projector is a reliable mainstay in reading instruction at the elementary school level. This device enlarges pages from a storybook, encyclopedia and dictionary. Likewise, when close study is desirable, it makes examination of pupil outlines, summaries and book reports more effective.

Eye Training

The opaque projector can be a valuable device when employed for eye training. Most opaque projectors come equipped with pointers which assist pupils in practicing left-to-right eye movement. Projected reading materials should be in large type and in manuscript form for a more eye-catching presentation in teaching this skill. The important art of skimming can be exercised by utilizing these projected materials.

Library and Reference Skills

The opaque is ideal for teaching reference skills as well as acquainting the pupils with library procedures. Items like note cards, sample bibliographies and catalog cards can be the foundation for a stimulating library lesson when projected from the opaque.

Teaching Directions

An increasing number of teachers are finding the opaque projector most helpful for teaching pupils how to follow instructions. The teacher writes a series of commands on 5 x 8″ cards, which are placed on the stage of the opaque. The commands might be based on simple classroom procedures involving the distributing, utilizing and collecting of classroom materials. The pupils are expected to carry out these printed directions.

Visual Discrimination

The opaque is a dependable device for teaching visual discrimination. Pictures of objects which are either alike or different, are projected on the opaque; as for example, a series of pictures of dogs might be studied for similarities as well as differences. A variation of this technique is to project a series of pictures showing items whose names either begin or end with the same sound.

Realia

Besides printed materials, objects like stamps, coins, keys, marbles, rocks, etc., may be projected. Where physical items of this nature are an integral part of a story, spend some time after projection discussing the role of the object in the events of a story. This technique allows pupils to see that objects described in the stories *can* be and *are* real.

PRIMARY ACTIVITIES

Story Movie   Ask pupils to prepare paper movies. After reading a particularly interesting story, have each pupil make a series of drawings illustrating highlights and events based on the story. Paste the illustrated happenings together in the proper sequence. Lay the beginning of the paper movie on the projector stand and pull the panels through slowly while the pupil narrates the story. Most opaque projectors have a roller, making it easier to crank the material through.

Stuffed Storyland People   A most unique use of the opaque projector occurs when storyland characters are brought to life in the guise of stuffed dolls. The process begins with a storybook illustration (preferably a line drawing) which is enlarged by the opaque onto a large sheet of paper and outlined. The picture serves as a basis for a pattern. Two pieces of material must be cut from the pattern to form a front and back view of the character. Later, stuffing material, such as rags, cotton or felt, is placed between the two pieces of material and sewn or stapled together to complete the doll. Some of the patterns may be cut from flannel or felt material to add the extra dimension of touch.

The Mystery Picture   Read paragraphs that describe scenery, events or a personality. First, see if the class can identify the item in question. Then, assign a title. To complete the activity, secure a picture from a magazine or newspaper, for opaque projection, that approximately reflects what was described in the paragraph.

INTERMEDIATE ACTIVITIES

Visual Book Reports   Have pupil teams give book reports using pictures or drawings. One pupil can place the material on the stage of the projector and operate the machine while the other person does the oral narration of the report.

Instant Recall   Ask pupils to collect a series of pictures for the opaque projector. The pictures should be colorful, interesting and contain a great deal of information. Flash each pupil's illustration sample on the screen. Ask the class to study the picture carefully; then shut off the projector for several minutes. Have the class list as many details as they can remember on the chalkboard. Then turn the projector on again so that the illustration can be re-examined and compared with the pupils' recollection of details.

Find the Paragraph   Select a series of descriptive paragraphs or sentences from several children's stories. Type or print them on plain white paper and project them on the opaque. See if the class, from the verbal clues, can identify the story from which they came.

OVERHEAD PROJECTOR

The emphasis on the utilization in the elementary school of the overhead projector has been quite frequently confined to science, math and social studies. Actually, overhead transparencies can open up a wide path to learning in such areas of reading as vocabulary, phonics, word analysis, comprehension and re-call interpretation, just to name a few.

Teaching Phonetics

There are many applications of the overhead projector to the reading curriculum. It is the ideal vehicle for teaching phonetics; transparencies, copied from workbook originals created by the teacher, can be prepared, based on such basic phonics principles as teaching initial sound or matching rhyming words.

Word Recognition

Recognizing antonyms, homonyms and synonyms can be accomplished with the use of overlays. Newly learned vocabulary words may be kept on transparencies for instant use.

Determining Reading Levels

Perhaps the most striking way the overhead can be employed is to help the teacher determine the composition of class reading groups; i.e., as a means of placing pupils in their correct reading level. Transparencies are derived from selected passages from basal readers of varying levels of difficulty which are, in turn, read orally by pupils for placement purposes.

Speed of Reading

The overhead is an excellent speed-reading teaching aid. A transparency with an appropriate reading passage is first covered with opaque paper, then each line is uncovered at a rate controlled by the teacher.

Pupil Involvement

The overhead is a pupil participation teaching device. Pupils can work directly at the overhead, participating in dictionary, phonics and word recognition exercises.

Clarifying Written Assignments

The overhead may be used to explain directions for homework, class assignments and tests. Such a demonstration makes it easier for a child to understand more clearly what is desired by the teacher and allows the pupil to work independently.

Transparencies for Homework

Use inexpensive X-ray plastic sheets or low-cost acetates for occasional homework and class assignments. In this way, assignments can be corrected in the class, and everyone can profit immediately from the corrections being done right on the transparency itself.

Brain Teasers

Have pupils develop transparencies in the form of crossword puzzles, cartoon puzzlers and riddles. The subject matter for the puzzles could be vocabulary lists, descriptive phrases, and poetry culled from texts or library books. Old reading workbook exercises and used copies of children's magazines are perfect sources for easily made transparencies. This old, about-to-be-discarded material could also be the basis for inspiration for teacher and pupil puzzle originals.

PRIMARY ACTIVITIES

A Game Activity   On the chalkboard draw a ladder which will represent plateau levels of achievement. The next step is to prepare sets of transparencies based on the mastery of vocabulary lists or word recognition skills. When pupils recognize each word correctly, they climb another rung on the ladder. If they make a mistake, the climber falls off the ladder and goes to the remedial reading hospital.

Supply the Missing Word   Have the entire class make up short stories consisting of two or three paragraphs. See that the best stories are made into transparencies, but in the transition, leave out key words in the story. Later, when each story transparency is shown, ask the class to supply the missing words.

Creative Stories   After the class has read several stories, let them recount the events for an overhead transparency. At the primary level, it is advisable for children to dictate these events to the teacher. A variation of this activity is to have pupils create their own stories, which are recorded by the teacher on a transparency. In this way, each student contributes one or two ideas to the cooperative story line that is being evolved. After the composite transparency is completed, duplicated copies of the story may be distributed.

Optical Discrimination   Place a number of cutout letters, numbers and figures on the stage of the overhead. After the class has viewed these items for a few minutes, shut off the machine, rearrange them on the projector, and remove one of the objects. Then turn on the projector, and see if the class can identify the missing object.

INTERMEDIATE ACTIVITIES

Cartoons   Prepare transparencies of interesting cartoons. Block out the dialogue in the comic strip panel of a cartoon or the caption in a political cartoon.

Dramatizing Words   Use a transparency containing a list of descriptive vocabulary words or action terms from reading stories. With a felt marker, pen or grease pencil, circle random words that you would like children to know thoroughly. Ask pupils not only to *explain* the word circled, but also to *dramatize* it by means of pantomime or chalkboard sketches. After pupils have visualized the word, the teacher may read the dictionary definition.

FILMSTRIPS AND SLIDES

Filmstrips are ideally suited to the teaching of reading skills and the appreciation of literature. They are particularly valuable in introducing, reviewing and concluding reading units in basal readers. Filmstrips, besides being a most reliable aid in dispensing facts and ideas, are especially valuable for individualized reading and remedial programs.

Slides of 3¼ x 4″ were an audio-visual mainstay years ago, but today they are not too frequently utilized in our elementary classrooms. Yet, they still have immeasurable value in reading instruction, particularly in the area of teaching phonetics and graphically illustrating stories and characters. Color slides, preferably of 2 x 2″, are indispensable for acquainting pupils with settings and environments so important to the development of a story. Slides are versatile because they can be shown in any sequence and are not restricted to a predetermined order, as is the case with motion pictures and filmstrips.

Teaching and Re-teaching with Filmstrips

The filmstrip can be extremely helpful in explaining facts or describing events of a story. A teacher may stop a filmstrip at any point, or before its concluding frames, to hold a class discussion. An alert teacher will make sure the class has grasped clearly the significance of events made in the story. One advantage of filmstrips is that a filmstrip can be repeated if the class is uncertain of facts or developments in the story. Attention should also be given to the individual filmstrip previewer which is an excellent device for enrichment purposes and is especially effective for remedial reading.

Slide Project as Tachistoscope Device

A unique application of the 2 x 2″ slide projector is to use it as a tachistoscope. A series or combination of commercially-made and amateur slides, representing physical objects, symbols, words and situations, can be flashed on the screen for improving word recognition and visual discrimination, and, most important, improve the rate of reading speed. Most 2 x 2″ slide projectors have a speed control device. With this control, pictures may be flashed on the screen at a predetermined pace.

Teaching Sequential Order with Slides

The 2 x 2″ slide is an imaginative way of teaching sequential patterns. The first step in such a method is to show a series of slides that tell a complete story in a logical order. Later, rearrange these same slides in an entirely different sequence; then, project them for the class. Survey the pupils' reactions to the changes in sequence. Later, the teacher should permit pupil committees to use sets of slides to tell their own stories. Filmstrips can also be utilized to teach sequential organization, but unfortunately, as noted previously, they lack the flexibility of the 2 x 2″ slide, since they are arranged in a fixed order.

PRIMARY ACTIVITIES

Magic of Words   Use a filmstrip based on ancient myths or fables as the basis for an experiment in story telling. In the experiment, pupils are invited to change the descriptive names and alter events, characters or settings in stories just viewed. For example, Little Red Riding Hood could become Little Green Glove who meets Fiery Purple Dragon on her way to her grandmother's house. Encourage pupils to make colorful drawings of the story, and write dialogue for these new characters.

Tall Tales   After watching a filmstrip based on folk heroes such as Pecos Bill, Paul Bunyan or Stormalong, suggest that pupils create an original folk character as the central figure of a tale of their own.

Filmstrips with Oral Narration   Occasionally play accompanying non-captioned filmstrips, with pupil narration on a tape recorder.

Story Slides   Using a commercial story line filmstrip as a guide, have the pupils prepare an animated story strip on white drawing paper. If possible, make the series of drawings approximate the size of the regular 35mm filmstrip. The series of drawings or panels should contain visual highlights of the story and should be told in sequence. After several strips are made, cut slits in an old shoe box, and pull the animated slide through the slots.

INTERMEDIATE ACTIVITIES

Filmstrip Evaluation   If two versions of a familiar children's story are available, show these differing versions and follow up with a class discussion. Discuss the merits and effectiveness of both filmstrips. Attention can be given to sequence, vocabulary and illustrative content of the slidefilm.

Teacher-Pupil Preview Committees   Invite two or three pupils from time to time to help the teacher preview filmstrips before showing to the entire class. Encourage the small committees to offer suggestions for its utilization as well as suggestions for class activities.

Introducing a New Unit   In reading, as with filmstrips, a carefully arranged set of slides from commercial or non-professional sources could familiarize children with physical objects in their own or in a distant, or foreign environment. For example, slides showing skyscrapers of New York, such as the Empire State Building, are an ideal introduction to a story about a big city.

"Word Bingo" "Word Bingo" is basically a word association activity and calls for a set of slides to be devised from reading vocabulary lists. Each time a slide picture illustrates a word on a pupil's "Bingo" list, the word is covered by the pupil until a series of recognized words in diagonal, horizontal or vertical pattern is blocked out and the lucky student having these words has "Word Bingo!"

Story Lantern Slides With a pinch of imagination and a dash of artistic skill, the $3\frac{1}{4}$ x 4″ slide can again be an effective visual aid in the reading program. Colorful lantern slides may be traced or copied from illustrations of a storybook, or pupils may wish to originate illustrated slides of their own based on creative impressions inspired by an appealing story they have read. Information on the production of original lantern slides can be found in John E. Morlan's *Preparation of Inexpensive Teaching Materials,* published by Chandler Publishing Company, San Francisco; De Kieffer and Cochran's *Manual of Audio-Visual Techniques,* published by Prentice-Hall of Englewood Cliffs, New Jersey; and G. E. Hamilton's *How to Make Homemade Lantern Slides,* published by the Keystone View Company, Meadville, Pa.

MOTION PICTURES

The 16mm sound motion picture media has an inherent visual attractiveness which is of special value in teaching reading. The various techniques employed to produce a motion picture can be used to teach such pertinent reading skills as understanding sequential order, furnishing the right atmosphere, recalling details, interpreting facts and predicting outcomes.

Time Concepts

If a basal reader is used, new units may be preceded with a movie that is relative to the topic. In other words, motion pictures are an excellent means for establishing time concepts, familiarizing pupils with the customs and costumes of specific groups of people and capturing the historical flavor of past events.

An Attractive Story Medium

The motion picture is an ideal medium for teaching the techniques of story telling. Familiarize your students with the basic elements that go into the production of a film. Discuss with the class the role of casting, settings, costumes, story continuity, direction, color, sound and music in the unfolding of a story on the screen.

Research and Motion Pictures

Film re-enactments of classic children's stories may also be compared with the original story. There have been numerous versions of such tales as *Three Musketeers, Tom Sawyer, Treasure Island, Black Beauty* and *Heidi*. Full-length films and specially edited versions of these classics are available to schools. Despite extensive research, some movie producers tamper with the plot and original premise of the author for so-called dramatic license. It is interesting to analyze a movie based on such classics. Numerous research activities can be the outgrowth of this technique.

Motion Pictures and Mental Imagery

Teachers should utilize motion pictures for exercises in mental imagery. For instance, project for the class a portion of a film with an interesting story line up to a climactic point, then run the film with the sound track only. After the film is finished, have the children attempt to describe what they thought took place in the unseen segment of the film. It will be interesting to see what mental pictures are conjured up in their minds after hearing the sounds. Run the film with picture and sound a second time in order to ascertain the accuracy of their mental imagery. A variation of this method is to run a film based on a familiar story with the sound shut off. Have several children take turns narrating the movie as it is being viewed. An exercise of this nature gives pupils drill in sequence and re-call and provides practice in comprehension.

PRIMARY ACTIVITIES

Coming Attractions   Have a committee of pupils prepare colorful posters, based on movie theater lobby displays, advertising the film. Some members of the committee might make stick figure cartoon stills or more sophisticated drawings of events in the film.

Most Unforgettable Character   After showing a motion picture version of an appealing story, ask pupils to write a short description or make a sketch based on the character in the tale who particularly fascinates them.

INTERMEDIATE ACTIVITIES

Capsule Film Critique   Have the class prepare short film reviews about film dramatizations of classic stories. Suggest to the class a rating system similar to the newspaper and magazine criteria.

Story Analysis When showing motion pictures, divide the class into committees, and have each committee report on a specific segment of the film. The objective of the activity is to provide children with experience in reporting key details and events in a motion picture.

Class-Evolved Motion Pictures Why not produce your own film version based on a classic reading story? Borrow or rent an inexpensive 8mm motion picture camera. Teachers do not have to be professional cameramen to produce a class film. Most of today's 8mm cameras are semi- or fully automatic. For basic camera techniques for amateur film makers, Eastman Kodak's *How to Make Good Movies* is suggested. A trip to the local camera store for information would be valuable. Depending on the age of the group, parent cooperation, and facilities of the school, let children become involved in all pertinent phases of motion picture productivity, such as writing the script, designing costumes and sets, and acting. As noted, the very mechanics of producing the motion picture helps to teach and reinforce reading skills. (See Figures 2-2, 2-3 and 2-4.)

Figure 2-2
Action Camera!

Figure 2-3
Make-Up Time

Figure 2-4
Practice Makes Perfect

Setting the Stage   During the initial period of producing the motion picture, instruct the pupils to set the stage for the entire story. The stage setting will indicate the mood of the story. A story in print, in describing a setting, appeals to the imagination, as contrasted to a motion picture wherein the setting is actually shown and nothing is left to the imagination. Why not encourage students, after reading a story, either to write a paragraph or sketch a picture which describes the setting? Later, show a film version of the same story. Invite comparison by the class on how well the motion picture depicts the setting of the story as originally described in the book.

History of Words   Try to arrange for the class to view a motion picture program from a foreign country. Have the class jot down interesting vocabulary peculiar to the country. Discuss with the class foreign words that we have borrowed from other countries, such as kindergarten, siesta, etc. Research on how words originated can be a fabulous language arts experience for children. Such a vocabulary activity could be extended to other subject areas, with films based on varying topics.

TEXTUAL AND PRINTED MATERIALS

A well-balanced reading program consists mainly of textual materials which should be supplemented and embellished with the positive learning values of the audio-visual media. Printed and textual materials are the spark for initiating creative activities, which in turn provide additional experiences in interpreting, clarifying, understanding, visualizing, summarizing and organizing.

Reading for a Purpose

Textbooks and other printed materials should be employed to help pupils develop a greater degree of skill in comprehending, interpreting and locating information. A teacher should give thoughtful reading assignments, ones that require pupils to skim, to assimilate information and understand the thoughts on the printed page. Pupils must be given experience in locating information through the effective utilization of the table of contents and the index. Alert teachers will also prepare question and activity exercises to help guide pupils through the important phases of reading.

The reading of one form of textual material whets the student's appetite for more information which can only be realized by further reading of other printed material. The ability to read is a vital necessity in doing research, and research makes reading a vital necessity.

Stimulating Thoughtful Class Discussions

Textbooks, library and reference materials can be the basis for class discussions. Pupils, after reading library books, should examine the viewpoints and themes of several texts on the same subject as well as analyzing different parts of the same book.

An Ever Increasing Vocabulary

New books are a source of a pupil's ever expanding vocabulary. Pupils should be shown how words and the contents in a book are clues to what a word means. They should be frequently stimulated to be on the lookout for new words in the books they read.

The Printed Word Comes Alive

Textbook materials in reading will be more meaningful if they are used in concert with other audio-visual media. What is described in print will come alive if the pupils' apperceptive background is augmented by the vicarious experiences supplied through the implements of audio-visual media.

PRIMARY ACTIVITIES

Role Playing   Select three or four main characters from an interesting story. Have pupils enact the role of the main characters. Later, have pupils switch their parts. The teacher may assist pupils in analyzing personality and motivation of the characters in the stories.

"The Further Adventures of . . ." After completing an imaginative story with colorful main characters, have children make up playlets that depict the further adventures or exploits of these appealing characters.

Paper Plate People On inexpensive paper plates, let the children draw faces that show a wide range of human emotions. Give these paper plate faces alliterative names, such as "Surprised Sue" or "Happy Horton." Next, prop these figures on the chalkboard shelf. Above the paper plates, the teacher can write descriptive phrases taken from a recently completed story. The trick is to have pupils read the descriptive phrases that identify the phrase.

Story Interpretation Select a story from a text or library book. Ask pupils to prepare a recounting of the story through their own eyes, as well as through the eyes of a key character, a bystander and a reporter. Later, have a student share his account with his classmates.

INTERMEDIATE ACTIVITIES

Translating Diacritical Marks Select a three- to four-sentence paragraph from a story, and write each on the chalkboard. As word-for-word, phonetically diacritical marks are shown, ask the class to translate the phonetic diacritical sentences into the correct form normally recognized; for example, "The wĕth ēr 'fōr kast ĭz 'pär shăl ly 'kloud ī skīz wĭth sŭm cháns ŏv līt 'shou ērz ĭn the 'ēv nĭng." A variation of this activity is to have pupils transpose statements from their regular form to the diacritical form.

Dialogue with a Story Character Let pupils select an appealing character from one of the stories they have read. Later, have them write an imaginary conversation between the character and themselves, about topics of interest to children of their age.

It Pays to Advertise Ask pupils to make up an advertisement for a book. Have them draw a picture to accompany the ad and also write a blurb for the dust cover.

Discussion Periods After a story has been read, ask the pupils to react to the way the author concludes his story. Would they have ended it the same way? Comment on how the author develops the characters in the story. Contrast the personalities of the main characters of a story as well as their needs and attitudes.

THE BULLETIN BOARD

The main objective of the bulletin board in reading is to motivate interest in good literature. Really effective bulletin boards will direct the pupil's attention to specific books, newspapers and magazine articles. Functional bulletin boards teach phonic skills, help pupils recall events and display students' achievements in storytelling and poetry. What a pupil reads and the progress he has made can be dutifully and attractively recorded on the bulletin board.

Defining Bulletin Board Objectives

It is a wise procedure, prior to setting up a bulletin board, for the classroom teacher to explain the theme or purpose of a desired bulletin board. The teacher should also allow a thorough class discussion of the objectives of the topics to be publicized.

Pupil Committee and Planning

Bulletin boards would probably be more successful if there were a greater degree of pupil participation in their planning and setting up. Why not use a committee approach in planning your next bulletin board?

A survey of pupils' cumulative folders should provide clues to their interests, aptitudes and proficiency in specific subject areas. Information gained in such a way should prove helpful in setting up pupil committees and guidelines for the selection of potential, attractive topics of study. Another source of information could be an informal questionnaire, distributed to students in the early days of the school term, in which they are queried on their hobbies and other interests. Most teachers, after four or five weeks, can generally recognize the pupils with leadership qualities and use them as the nucleus for the various groups. It is wise to keep pupil committees' sizes down to a manageable level of from three to five students. Pupil committees should be balanced by a pupil who verbalizes well, another who has reasonably good command of written language and enjoys research, and perhaps one who is creatively endowed.

Eye-Catching Bulletin Boards

Books and short stories might be publicized by using unique art forms to direct attention to bulletin boards. On a bulletin board dealing with a completed story theme, why not supplement a pupil's drawing and composition with a mobile that recreates appealing characters and interesting objects from the story? Clothespin puppets or pipe cleaner figures could also be utilized to colorfully depict characters featured on bulletin board displays.

Geographic Backdrop

Outline maps make an interesting backdrop for bulletin board displays. Locations mentioned in books or stories the class has read could be circled on the map. The interest in these locations could be used to stimulate further interest in reading about the geographic areas where stories take place.

Vocabulary Staging Area

The bulletin board is just the right vehicle for expanding the pupil's vocabulary activities. Use the technique of mystery or curiosity to accomplish this. For example, a large, animated figure on the bulletin board could be looking for words to complete a series of sentences, the pupils, of course, being the suppliers of missing terms. The bulletin board also serves as a staging area or clearing house for all newly acquired vocabulary words.

PRIMARY ACTIVITIES

"Polly the Parrot"   Have the children draw a series of colorful, intelligent-looking parrots. Draw a colorful parrot on strong cardboard or reinforced oaktag. For each parrot, insert a cuphook beneath his bill. As new words are learned or met by pupils for the first time, have pupils write the word on a 3 x 5" card which has a small hole punched through it. Attach each word on the cuphook, and have others in the class guess the pronunciation and meaning of the word. Words on the cuphooks can be used for review purposes; multi-colored parrots could represent different reading groups in the class.

Storyland Characters Spring to Life   Prepare a large construction paper silhouette simulating a library book. Have students prepare line drawings of their favorite storybook characters, such as Tom Sawyer or Mary Poppins, in either a standing or walking position. Place the drawn figures so that they appear to be exiting from the book moving into the center of the bulletin board display.

Doll Displays   This will appeal to the young ladies in the class. Dolls, especially such historical types as colonial or pioneer dolls, make stimulating displays when attractively arranged and combined with other real objects. These doll displays make a timely tie-in with readings dealing with colonial or pioneer themes.

INTERMEDIATE ACTIVITIES

Storybook Dioramas Literature provides pupils with an unlimited source of ideas for dioramas which can be based on real or fictional people, and imagined or historical incidents. The simplest diorama is the shoebox type. Scenery can be either drawn or made from construction paper. Easy-to-handle pipe cleaners and cardboard cutouts make uncomplicated story people. Dioramas based on the Civil War, space exploration, medieval days and prehistoric times are sure-fire subjects for boys at the elementary level.

Timely Bulletin Boards One of the big problems with bulletin boards is to keep them from getting stale. Why not use a huge cowboy construction paper figure with a lasso on a bulletin board? Within the lasso place written book reports or reviews; later, replace the résumés with pupils' drawings depicting highlights from a completed story.

Book Salesman Allow a pupil or a small committee to arrange an attractive bulletin board and display of interesting books. Have one of the members of the committee act as a book salesman and try to have him persuade others to buy his book.

Bookfair Arrange a class bookfair where bulletin boards will display drawings, models and dioramas highlighting some of the books enjoyed by the class.

Unique Book Report Display Ask pupils to imagine that they are some of the important characters from their favorite story. In this activity, the pupils, representing storybook characters, actually write letters to other storyland characters discussing adventures in their respective stories. For example, Heidi might be corresponding with Tom Sawyer and Huckleberry Finn, or Long John Silver of *Treasure Island* might be exchanging pleasantries with Captain Ahab of *Moby Dick*. Simple sketches of storybook characters should be an integral part of the letters. The illustrated letters would make an attractive bulletin board display.

THE FLANNEL BOARD

Flannel boards are a reliable device for providing a significant beginning for dramatizing stories and reviewing events in teaching phonetic elements. Free or inexpensive cutouts from old workbooks and magazines, or simple children's drawings placed on cardboard and then backed with felt or flannel material, are inexpensive tools for dramatizing stories.

The following techniques are to be recommended for effecting more absorbing and dramatic flannel board story presentations:

Visualizing Story Dramatization

Flannel board pictures are mainly used to assist children in following the plot of a story or as a technique in which children are called upon to speculate about future events in the story. Depending on the maturity of the group, allow pupils to select stories for flannel board dramatization. Not all stories lend themselves to the visual telling medium of the flannel board. Stories selected should make each child in the class feel he is part of the story.

Sequence of Events

Use flannel cutouts to represent pertinent storybook characters and pose questions about these characters. Questions about the story should be arranged in sequence so that a systematic review of the story takes place while pupils are also gaining valuable experience in oral and written expression (Figure 2-5).

Practice Makes Perfect

A final piece of advice calls for the teacher or pupil narrator in the storytelling exercise to have some practice in telling the story before he dramatizes it in front of the class.

Teaching Phonetic Skills

Besides story re-enactments the flannel board is a helpful means of teaching phonics skills. For example, one set of blank 3 x 5" or 5 x 8" index cards is needed, on which pre-selected words on one idea are printed with a felt marker or black crayon. The cards are then "backed" with the correct felt or flannel material. Place on the flannel board three or four sets of 3 x 5" vocabulary cards containing the like phonetic elements or characteristics. The sets should be arranged in a mixed pattern on the flannel board. Allow the class to study the words a few minutes; then have pupils use colored yarn to visually connect the words with similar characteristics.

PRIMARY ACTIVITIES

Ardent Conversationalist Have two pupils manipulate flannel board with selected figures, as in a puppet activity. A good idea is to allow

Courtesy of Instructo, Paoli, Pa.

Figure 2-5

Flannel Board Story Sequence Kit

Kits of this type will help children develop sequential understanding by manipulating the colorful cutouts.

pupils to have the characters move about on the board and enjoy a full-blown conversation.

Classification Activity Place on the board a simple flannel-backed picture of tractors on a farm in the country. After showing a picture object, ask the class to list other things they would find in the country.

Phonetic Recognition To increase skills in perceiving similarities and differences in sounds, place on the flannel board a series of magazine and newspaper pictures where four out of five items begin with the same initial consonant sound. Ask the class if they can find the object with the *different* sounds.

SUMMARY

Generally, audio-visual instructional materials have not achieved their full potential as effective learning aids in the teaching of reading.

No educator will dispute the fact that reading is a basic skill subject—the key which helps unlock all learning in other curriculum areas. Why not utilize audio-visual aids to achieve a greater mastery of skills in reading? Remember, whether the audio-visual instructional aid is an old standby such as the chalkboard, bulletin or flannel board, or one of the more appealing newer ones like the overhead projector, each serves the ultimate objectives of making reading more enjoyable, inspirational, and above all, more meaningful to all elementary classroom pupils, regardless of their ability.

3

AUDIO-VISUAL TECHNIQUES FOR IMPROVING WRITTEN AND ORAL EXPRESSION

It is truly amazing, the adaptability of the tape recorder in practically all of the written or oral language curricular programs. In addition to being the logical vehicle for detecting and correcting incorrect speech patterns, the tape recorder is the ideal audio tool for developing dramatic skills, preparing assemblies, executing oral discussion activities, and improving listing and note-taking ability via dictation. To complement the effectiveness of the tape recorder, teachers are free to use such inexpensive and easy-to-operate audio devices as disc recordings and AM-FM radio. As with the tape recorder, records and radio can provide the classroom teacher with unlimited means of developing creative techniques and activities in written and oral expression.

The utilization of such graphics as magazine illustrations, cartoon panels, study prints, snapshots, charts and posters opens an exciting and relatively low-cost avenue to teaching skills in language creativity to our pupils. Graphics are best utilized as a catalyst for stirring pupils' imaginations—too often teachers take for granted this readily accessible visual tool.

Both the opaque and overhead are key tools to the classroom teacher in pursuit of effective written language. The opaque can be used as an instructional extension of graphics materials with the added obvious advantage of enlargement. These two projection devices allow pupil and teacher to study well written language samples and compare them to those which are poorly written. The latter can be corrected on the spot. The element of immediacy is an obvious advantage with these two instructional aids.

Many of the advantages of filmstrips and slides involved with teaching reading skills can be applied readily to instruction in written or oral language. These visual tools are ideal devices for stimulating pupils' imaginations in composition work, writing titles, captions and quotations, and above all, they give the teacher an additional method of teaching sequential understanding and classification skills which are so vital in written expression. Finally, both filmstrips and slides serve to visually clarify concepts and seek to prevent confusion and misinterpretation of facts and information.

Motion pictures, with all the instructional attributes and visual attractiveness of both filmstrips and slides, feature the added impact of sound. This aural advantage is most important in teaching skills in observation, and it supplies an audio-visual frame of reference for research and other pertinent writing activities. Much of what can be said about film techniques and activities can be applied to language instruction with television.

Sometimes teachers may not consider dramatization as an audio-visual tool. The use of the human voice and body is one of man's earliest forms of audio-visual communication. Dramatics, as a teaching device, cannot be relegated exclusively to a solitary role in the English curriculum; it can be correlated with other curriculum areas, be they reading, science, math or social studies.

TAPE RECORDER, RECORDS AND RADIO

Record for Dramatic Performance

The tape recorder acts as an audio mirror to children's vocal performances. The classroom teacher could be relieved from casting roles in play tryouts by simply having the class record the parts on tape, then allow the group to vote on the pupil who performed the best in each dramatic part.

As noted in Chapter 2, pupils' cumulative folders are a rich source of information, especially the previous teachers' comments and grades for oral expression. Obviously, experiences in various oral activities such as class discussions, oral book reports and pantomime activities should give the alert teacher insight into the child's poise and ability to communicate with his classmates. No formal dramatic activity should be undertaken until the term is well under way and the teacher well-acquainted with each pupil's oral abilities.

Memorization Technique for Class Plays

Learning lines for a play, skit or lines for choral reading can be made easier by taping selected passages and playing them over and over again until the lines are mastered. This can be done on a group or individualized basis. Students working with this tape technique usually develop a superior ability to memorize.

Tape Recording and Puppetry

Puppet plays and pantomime can also be enhanced by the tape recorder. In both dramatic activities, record the entire playlet on tape and have the children manipulate their puppets or pantomime the words to the recording.

Audio Tool for Speech Diagnosis and Therapy

The tape recorder can do much to improve every child's speech. If used intelligently it can be utilized to identify and provide corrective speech measures. Of course, the classroom teacher is not a speech therapist, but he can, by making available to the speech therapist a tape of a natural conversation of a child who may be having speech difficulty, assist in the diagnosis and formulation of the prescription for remedial correction.

Teaching Vowel and Consonant Sounds

This audio device may be employed to help pupils learn individualized letter, vowel and consonant sounds. Why not utilize the appeal of color and sense-of-touch materials such as felt, wood, clay and brick, together with aural sounds supplied by the recorder, to differentiate various sounds? Another technique is to have the teacher prepare a series of tapes, saying aloud short and long vowels or words with appropriate pauses which will permit the pupil to select the correct visual to associate with the sound or word. Still another suggested technique is the use of pastel color illustrations or drawings to visually represent soft vowel sounds being heard on the tape.

Creative Oral Grammar

Oral grammar exercises, usually considered a drudge to both teacher and pupil, can be made more attractive through the recorder. Drill can be executed with a creative flair in such areas as in the utilization of nouns, verbs and adjectives, enunciation, verb tense, and agreement of subject and predicate. For example, to improve pupil response, prepare a series of sentences in which a certain language pattern may be followed and allow the pupils, either on paper or orally, to supply the missing items.

Tapes for Dictation and Listening

In written language the tape recorder may be used for dictation and note-taking purposes. When dictating to students, space your speech narration to allow pupils sufficient time for writing and avoiding lengthy paragraphs. The recorder, being a dynamic aural tool, will make pupils better listeners and, likewise, better note-takers with a greater degree of accuracy and fluency.

Commercial Tapes for Language Art Lessons

Tapes taken from radio, or secured from the National Tape Repository at Boulder, Colorado, or the audio portion of television or commercial recordings, can be utilized, as was the case in the related area of reading, to dramatize famous children's classics for literary appreciation. Dramatization is an excellent incentive for creative writing exercises.

Records Motivate Language Expression

There is an increasing number of imaginative commercial recordings highly adaptable for improvement and development of oral and written language skills. We can use records to spur interest, to supply content to a language lesson by providing effective re-creations of fictional narratives and realistic experiences, and most important, to provide a catalyst in the area of creative writing by establishing the proper mood through setting.

Records for Language Enrichment

There are some excellent records released which are ideal for language arts activities as incentives for background in activities for creative writing and poetry. For example, the services of such famed actors as Ed Begley, Boris Karloff, Cyril Ritchard, Judith Anderson, Carol Channing, Walter Brennan and Edward G. Robinson have dramatized and narrated such classics as *Evangeline, Tom Sawyer, Man Without a Country,* Kipling's *Jungle Books, Madeline* and *A Child's Garden of Verses.* (All are produced by Caedmon Records, Inc., 505 8th Avenue, New York.)

Records and Poetry

Teachers should not hesitate to use professional recordings of good children's poetry, or to ask children to develop their own poems and other simple prose that follow the pattern, rhythm and rhyme of the originals they have heard. An interesting form of record utilization to stimulate children's poetry is *Miracle Poems Written by Children,* recorded by

Julie Harris and Roddy Mc Dowell on Caedmon Records and used by a number of creative teachers in several Long Island schools.

Records and Creative Writing

Like the popular recording "In the Mood," why not put your pupils in the proper creative writing mood with music? Use recordings like Tschaikowsky's "Nutcracker Suite" or Dukas' "Sorcerer's Apprentice" as motivational mood music for a stimulating writing session. Allow children to write down the thoughts imagined and words that come to their minds before they begin an actual composition. Lively class discussions and listing of words on the chalkboard will add spice and be a constructive guideline to their writing.

Radio and Language Arts Skills

Once, Mark Twain made an amusing comment about his premature obituary, in a cable from Europe to the Associated Press, in which he said, "Reports of my death are greatly exaggerated." The story of educational radio's death was similarly "greatly exaggerated." Like its aural counterparts, the tape recorder, disc records, and educational radio can be an emphatic force in language instruction in literature. Radio sparks the enrichment cycle, readily fostering good listening and speaking skills, and furthers appreciation of literature and dramatization.

Educational Radio

The most effective educational radio program is WNYE-FM, sponsored by the New York Board of Education, which provides member schools with a comprehensive radio manual replete with teaching suggestions and pupil classroom activities to preface and enrich the language arts programming.

Radio as a Pattern for Improving Vocabulary

Radio can be used as a means to improve a student's language and speech patterns, vocabulary, pronunciation and sentence structure. Appropriate well-stimulated programs can help to teach outlining and sequential patterns in language arts.

Radio and Language Activity

Good educational broadcasts encourage young listeners to examine their own experiences and write more readily and imaginatively about them. Commercial and educational broadcasts have the advantage of realistic sound and musical effects. Well-selected programs can be a dynamic impetus to varied language arts activities.

Inspirational and Imaginative Radio Dramatizations

If the subject matter on a tape is known in advance, have pupils bring in articles, photos or any material related to the topic. Encourage pupils to listen to story and information programs or current events as a means of leading into exciting classroom debates and discussions. Programs based on myths and legends can be an incentive to do research for bulletin board activities by class committees.

PRIMARY LEVEL AUDIO ACTIVITIES

Drama Workshop   Have pupils dramatize on tape a stimulating and imaginative situation, such as reporting the launching of an astronaut to the moon; or have pupils enact realistic situations, such as calling a friend or reporting an emergency to the doctor, fire or police departments.

Planning Experience   When the children are planning plays or programs, particularly for special occasions such as Halloween and Christmas, arrange to record the actual planning of decisions and ideas; play the tape back as an audio reminder of what was decided by the group.

Identification   Either the pupil or teacher can tape descriptions of objects such as fruit or furniture, and have the class identify these objects.

Guess the Word   Have children write a word with its phonetic spelling and a sentence which deals with the picture. Later, have each pupil record this sentence and the class try to guess the word; or make a list of vocabulary words that go along with the verbal descriptions.

"Sharing Time"   Primary level children love "Show and Tell" sessions, so why not prepare "Sharing Time" on tape? Then arrange these recordings and evaluate with the class. It is interesting to compare with the class this tape session with that made later on.

INTERMEDIATE AUDIO ACTIVITIES

Committee Dramatizations   Divide the class into committees, and have teams perform playlets on simple themes. Have the class vote on the best story and best performance.

Public Address Announcements   Have students prepare an announcement for the March of Dimes, Community Chest, Salvation Army and other public services and charities, and offer these spot announcements to local radio facilities. If this is impractical, arrange to use the public address system for announcements of class activities and newsworthy items involving class members and their families.

"Sound Off"   After a pupil has prepared an original composition or poem, have him tape his work. Later, play the entire tape of stories and poems and help pupils draw comparisons from what they wrote on paper as contrasted to the way the same story sounded orally.

Radio vs. Newspapers   Pep up current events and class discussion sessions by having pupils listen to radio broadcasts and compare their articles with the way news commentators analyze the same events. This is an activity directed to more sophisticated and well-read students at the upper intermediate level.

Creative Radio Scripts   Have pupils develop their own radio scripts for taping. The teacher should initiate the discussion of suitable topics, but elicit from the children other subjects as well; then guide them in writing scripts and eventually tape the scripts. For example: (1) Interview the President or other important personalities. (2) Interview a Martian who just arrived from outer space. (3) Discuss the danger of water and air pollution.

GRAPHICS IN ENGLISH

The prime objective of a language program is to improve both oral and written communication. In either, a subject-matter-centered curriculum or experience-centered program, pictures, posters and charts can successfully assist in the instruction of English.

Pictures Set the Mood

Pictures establish a mood. A classroom with carefully chosen graphics enables children to relax and become interested, and there is a greater ease to communicate orally.

Graphics Enhance Pupils' Written and Oral Expression

In reading, pictures and related graphics are used to enhance story-telling. Students deliver oral reports or talks more fluently when helped by an available resource file of pictures. Illustrative material assists the speaker in coveying his ideas, creates interest in his topic, and above all, sets the stage for the talk.

One area in which graphics can be most useful is speech therapy. Carefully chosen pictures, incorporated into well-planned speech exercises, help the self-conscious pupil forget his handicap since he is absorbed in relating the story of pictures and identifying objects in illustrations—in a sense, providing appropriate captions for photographs.

Graphics for Reference

Picture files are most helpful in researching class dramatic productions. Their use supplies visual information for capturing feelings and states of mind. They also act as a reference point for recreating authentic scenery and dress. A file of materials, collected by teacher and pupils, should increase as the year progresses.

Graphics Clarify Language Expression

As is the case in oral language, graphic charts and simple drawings can make composition and other forms of written expression more effective when incorporated in a written assignment at appropriate places. Any form of illustration may serve to motivate interest and clarify written expression.

Pictures Stimulate a "Thousand Words"

An oft quoted remark is, "What's in a picture?" It is significant that the dictionary uses drawings and pictures to clarify meanings of words. Such pictorial material as magazine illustrations, cartoons, study and art prints, picture postcards and photographs, can be used to stimulate children in creative talk and writing, as well as to clarify vocabulary. Large study prints are also proving to be an excellent visual device in encouraging verbalization through class discussion.

Graphics Teaching Outlining and Sequence

Outlining and story sequence is a difficult concept to convey to children in elementary grades. Large magazine illustrations, cartoon panels, postcards and photographs are ideal visual devices when arranged on the bulletin board or flannel board to teach key concepts in story development and reports.

Abstract Art and Creative Expression

The utilization of appropriate marginal illustrations makes ideal motivational devices for inspiring creative drawings. The classroom teacher, with the art specialist's cooperation, can help children devise abstract sketches or simple line drawings and colorful paintings which could serve as a basis for imaginative excursions in written language.

Graphics and Bulletin Board Research

Interesting bulletin board displays of photographs and other illustrative material may be used to pose provocative questions which could lead to interesting research projects.

Experiences for Primary Children

Many children, especially at the primary level, find it extremely difficult to write without some incentive or frame of reference. Appropriate flat pictures can identify familiar objects, bridging the gap between the known and unknown (or from the simple to the complex) and give sense to new words and terms.

Graphics Assist Children in Interpretation

Pictures help children interpret what they see, assist them in comparing distance, shapes and sizes; also they provide practice in selecting titles for stories and in writing captions.

Graphics Resource Files

Teachers should start picture files on attractive topics. They should select pictures that are typical rather than unusual. For example, pictures on the bulletin of Africa should avoid the stereotypes such as dancing natives, and should instead convey an accurate and authentic impression of the subject, thus providing children with the right kind of vicarious experience for writing.

Symbols and Expression

The animal beast responds and is *conditioned* by signals and symbols, but man *thinks* mainly with his symbols. How each being interprets those symbols may not be the same. Why not employ unusual word symbols as the catalyst for inspired class discussions and imaginative forms of writing prose and poetry? Appropriate study prints and other graphics, plus motion pictures, can set the stage for a story of the seasons, a science fiction story or Halloween tale.

Flat Pictures Develop Skills in Interpretation

Flat pictures are an instrument to familiarize primary children in recognizing names of objects. Later, as children mature, graphics help children develop a degree of interpretation about movement, location, touch, sound and color. Pupils begin to relate experiences and previous learning, the result being more fluent speakers and writers.

The end result of the pictorial technique in writing and speaking is developing the ability of children to draw inferences and predict outcomes.

PRIMARY GRAPHICS ACTIVITIES

Start a Story   Have the class break up into groups. Taking one group at a time, give the first child a picture image, and have him start a story and pass the picture along to the next person in his group. Each must add to the story until the picture reaches the last person in the group, who tries to supply an interesting conclusion.

Instant Words   Encourage pupils to draw pictures that illustrate nouns and action verbs. Later, have the children illustrate descriptive words and pictures. The culmination of this activity would have students label and caption these illustrative materials.

Finding Synonyms   Select a series of photographs or related pictures which show a word and ask the class to find old magazine pictures and postcards that are either synonyms or antonyms for the words highlighted.

Picture Pantomime   Show a series of photographs illustrating actions and have pupils pantomime or make up short playlets from what they have observed in the illustrations.

Establish the Mood   Supply the pictures yourself to illustrate moods such as anger, sadness, happiness, etc. Or ask the class to collect their own material for this objective.

Rhyme the Time   Initiate a rhyming word chart inspired by a series of selected pictures that conjure up words that rhyme: for example, a picture of *rain* calls to mind such words as stain, Spain, lane, pane, etc.

INTERMEDIATE GRAPHICS ACTIVITIES

Nonsense Stories   An imaginative activity involving modern art techniques is to have pupils make abstract figures with crayon or paint. These bizarre drawings can serve as a basis for nonsense poems or stories.

Footprints on the Ceiling   The teacher could make a series of footprints on construction paper, before class, attach them (possibly with pressure sensitive tape) in a progression, up the walls to the ceiling. When the class does arrive, have the children write a short paragraph to explain these strange footprints. Could the prints belong to a pink elephant or to some other strange creature?

Creative Writing Packets   Place old postcards, mystery illustrations and cartoon panels in an envelope and have pupils prepare a story. Primary pupils could be assisted in this undertaking by placing in the envelope key vocabulary words along with the individual picture packet.

Comic strips and single panel cartoons can help teach pupils quotation marks. Have students take one such panel in which the conversation character's words are encased in balloons. Request that pupils transfer the cartoon character's speech into the form of a direct quotation.

Dictionary Practice   One of the key skills is the use of the dictionary. Use photographs and other illustrations depicting nouns and action verbs and direct students to look up words to fit the illustration.

Camera Club   Start a camera club, preferably at the fifth or sixth grade level. Students' cameras do not have to be expensive. The relatively inexpensive, easy-to-operate Instamatic cameras can be used for collecting a whole series of photographs of people, or for visually recording events such as field trips, to stimulate exercises in creative writing and reporting.

OPAQUE PROJECTOR

The Opaque Magnified for Effective Proofreading

The opaque is still a most reliable visual tool in teaching language reference skills for it can magnify pages in the dictionary, reference books, encyclopedia and almanac. It still is valuable for proofreading purposes and requires very little preparation on the teacher's part.

Opaque Correlates Well

The opaque and tape recorder can be used in concert for teaching poetry or choral reading purposes. For example, words can be printed on 5 x 8" cards and projected via the overhead; the tape recording can be synchronized with the printed material on the screen.

Opaque Commands Interest

The opaque projector can take the best features of graphics, and with its mighty lens, expand these graphics to an impressive and commanding size. Groups of children are able to supplement their oral reports and talks by combining the opaque with the tape recorder.

OPAQUE ACTIVITIES AT ALL LEVELS

Getting the Main Idea

On the chalkboard the teacher reads or writes several sentences. Later, on the opaque projector, he projects a series of pictures or illustrations, one of which best expresses the main idea in each sentence.

Creative Stories and Poetry

Have the class prepare simple line drawings of silly animals. Project these drawings on the screen, and ask the class to prepare limericks, poems and riddles on or about these crazy mixed-up animals. With the opaque, project pictures or drawings of seasonal activities, such as shoveling snow, ice skating and skiing in winter, which are excellent stimulants for written and oral language exercises.

THE OVERHEAD PROJECTOR

Overhead Excellent Proofreading Device

The overhead projector serves as a "magic lantern" for oral and written language instruction. The overhead is most effective in proof of composition performances, and teaching skills in outlining.

Improving Composition Skills

Like the opaque, the overhead projector is an excellent device for teacher-pupil analysis of composition; i.e., for correcting faults in grammar, selecting unnecessary words and analyzing sentence structure. Of course, pupil compositions and other language exercises can be viewed directly on the opaque projector without the need for preparing a transparency, but the improving techniques and ease of preparing professional transparencies must be recognized.

Opaque Materials on the Overhead

Opaque paper cutouts placed on the stage of the overhead projector give teachers and pupils more flexibility in their teaching of English. Students love to manipulate objects on the overhead, and if allowed to participate, their own attention and that of their classmates is assured. Use projected silhouettes (opaque cutouts) to dramatize stories for visual class discussion; other exciting learning activities can be stimulated by this technique.

Analyzing Written Assignments

A pupil's written assignments, when transferred to a transparency, make the topic truly one of class observation, in which the entire class is involved. The side effects are: more interest in written language assignments and encouragement of more legible and neater work, once pupils know it will be projected. When projected, a step-by-step analysis of the sentence structure is made. Original poems by pupils may be projected for discussion, and professional lines of poetry may be utilized in the interest of understanding of rhythm or rhyming poetry.

The Overhead Role in Research Activities

As with the opaque projector, transparencies may also be involved in teaching reference skills so necessary in research work. Transparencies can also be used to review and teach pertinent library terms, such as call numbers, classification of fiction, non fiction, etc. Copies of simple tables of contents and indexes can be readily made.

PRIMARY ACTIVITIES

Garbled Story Sequence   Elements in teaching story sequence in English have been successfully tried by enterprising teachers who employ a series of illustrated and colored acetates depicting key characters in a story in the order of their appearance. Later, these very same acetates are shown *out of sequence* in a deliberately garbled version of the story. This is an intriguing and challenging way to study the elements of story sequence in composition work.

Interesting Silhouettes   On the overhead stage, place such diverse objects as keys, pieces of paper, coins, checkers, and bottle caps, and survey the reaction of the children. Such objects should stimulate young imaginations for oral and written expression.

Memorization   The overhead can serve as a visual device to help children memorize poetry or lines of script, just as the tape recorder was an audio device to accomplish the same objective. Use opaque material to cover the selection and test the child's memory.

INTERMEDIATE ACTIVITIES

Illustrative Book Reports   Pupil-made overhead transparencies that illustrate sequences in a story on which they are reporting will heighten interest in often routine activity. The illustration can be made with a grease pencil. Several teachers have found that small, clear plastic bags may be cut to desired size and serve as an inexpensive transparency. Mounted transparencies, after reports are given, may be affixed to class windows.

Language Crossword Puzzles   Pupil-made crossword puzzle transparencies, with overlays, are an effective way to introduce lessons on synonyms, homonyms and antonyms. After experience with visual technique, and depending on the sophistication of the class, you may wish to use overlays.

Character-Setting-Plot Practice in developing topic sentences, main ideas and paragraphing position, with appropriate transparencies of selected passages of good children's stories, can help pupils see how professionals establish character, setting and plot. Then, after standards or guidelines for this event are set up, project transparencies of paragraphs from stories and reports. Explain in the exercise that a good topic sentence is judged by the sentences that follow.

Repetition To teach children the necessity for expanding their vocabulary and repeating the same thoughts and terms, prepare a transparency that contains repetitive and redundant, tiresome verbals. Ask the class to find appropriate synonyms to substitute for the overworked words.

FILMSTRIPS AND SLIDES

Effective Paragraph Writing

Filmstrips are excellent because of their simplicity of operation and are well suited to the teaching of paragraph writing. By using one or two frames at a time, the projector may be stopped, and the pupils asked to write short paragraphs describing what they viewed. An entire exercise in writing a story or report can be taught in this manner. The same technique can be utilized with films with a stop frame projector system.

A Vocabulary Enrichment Device

Most filmstrips are accompanied by simple, concise narratives and pupils can be encouraged to write substitute captions for the originals. Such a technique, with wise teacher guidance, becomes an excellent device for pupils to learn new vocabulary and to express themselves in other ways.

Motivating Class Discussion

Teacher-pupil committees could preview filmstrips and select either an issue, vocabulary list and phrases, or a series of facts as impetus to interesting class discussion and debates.

Follow-Up Projects

A subject area filmstrip would be more effective if followed by other meaningful experiences, such as well directed research projects, story writing and interesting worksheets.

Filmstrips Guide to Good Language Practices

Filmstrips, since they are made by professionals, provide ready-made samples of correct punctuation, correct usage and good sentence structure. Filmstrips may, of course, have dual purposes, not only teaching the mechanics of good English, but perhaps successfully correlating subject matter in such areas as science and social studies. For example, social studies filmstrips may be used to find words with the same beginnings, names and terms, which may be put in alphabetical order. Capitalization exercises and location of proper nouns are also readily adaptable from social studies and science filmstrip subjects for language arts purposes. In other words, most filmstrips, depending on their content, lend themselves easily to one type of English activity or another.

Flexibility of Slides in Language Instruction

The media of 35mm slides and 3¼ x 4″ slides have the distinct advantage of flexibility over filmstrips since slides can be shown in any order or sequence. This is particularly important in teaching specific sequential skills in writing. There is also an increasing tendency to use pupil- and teacher-narrated tapes to accompany slide presentations. This is an area of tremendous potential yet to be fully explored (Figure 3-1).

FILMSTRIP AND SLIDE ACTIVITIES AT ALL LEVELS

Class Language Resource File   The class could set up a file of 2 x 2″ slide transparencies which could be based on class activities such as interesting places children and teachers have visited. Duplicates of slides taken by pupils and parents, and some excellent commercial slides, could be used to illustrate talks. Good slides on science and social studies orientation topics will create an impetus toward creative writing and research.

Filmstrip Enrichment   Plan to follow film and filmstrip lessons by having children re-tell, in their own words, what they viewed and then create a series of word, phrase and sentence strips. A variation of this is a scrapbook of pupil illustrations, including drawings or magazine pictures to complement key sentences and phrases taken from the filmstrip.

Provide a Title   Have pupils, after viewing a filmstrip, work cooperatively in selecting titles and making up a story related to the filmstrip. The story may be recorded on the tape recorder or simply dramatized in class.

Courtesy of Eastman Kodak Company

Figure 3-1
Kodak Ektagraph Slide Projector

Filmstrip Sequential Story Telling   Don't throw away old torn film-strips. Instead, cut them up and use either a series of individual and related or unrelated frames as an activity in which pupils use these frames to tell an impromptu story or evolve a creative tale.

Filmstrip Writing Sessions   Try to secure a filmstrip with a pictur-esque landscape or background, ocean scene or countryside, as an in-centive for creative writing purposes.

Questioning Filmstrip   Have a committee of pupils select a story-type filmstrip for which the questions Who?, Why?, Where? or When? must be answered. Ask each pupil showing the filmstrip to answer these questions. Discuss differences between reading a story and viewing a film-strip.

MOTION PICTURES

Visual Imagery—Fiction vs. Truth

Films help pupils think more purposefully and creatively. They stimulate the imagination. Good films and effective teacher utilization assist pupils in discerning between fantasy and the truth. Films provide mental pictures in the pupil's mind, a visual imagery that undeniably helps a pupil to write with more expression, imagination, and objectivity.

Vocabulary and Grammar Skills

Films are visuals which supply vicarious experiences that motivate children to learn and work with new words. There is an unlimited wealth of films based on such key language topics as outlining, pronunciation, creative writing, word usage, dictionary skills, literature and vocabulary.

Film Sound Techniques in English Instruction

It is a known fact that most children's listening and speaking vocabulary is far more extensive than his actual reading vocabulary. For example, a science film on the housefly introduces terms like *pupa, proboscis* and *cilia*. Sound tracks of films provide children with new vocabulary terms and patterns for correct usage. There are films like Coronet's "Poems are Fun" which stimulate interest in poetry as well as choral reading. Films can also provide students with audio-visual material which is helpful in learning to write descriptions of incidents.

Interesting Experiences in Oral Language Expression

Sound films, in teaching reading, can be stopped at crucial points, or they can be run without the sound track turned on. They can be re-run a second and third time. This device of shutting off the sound provides children with experience in narrating, conversing, and reviewing key details and happenings.

Creative Films for Creative Writing

There are an increasing number of films available for creative writing sessions. One excellent film is McGraw-Hill's "Autumn Pastorale," with a musical sound track, devoid of spoken narration, that can act as a springboard for imaginative writing. Other inexpensive films, such as Weston Woods' "Sorcerer's Apprentice" and Contemporary Films' excellent animated film, "Clay," can also serve as a nucleus for stimulating written expression.

FILM ACTIVITIES AT ALL LEVELS

Problem Solving   Show a dramatic film that has a significant problem in which some key decision or judgment has to be rendered or resolved by one of the film's main characters. Ask the class what they would do if faced with the same problem.

Write the Producer   After seeing a particularly effective film, have the class write the producer, director, or one of the actors involved in making the film.

Film Discussion   Show a film such as "Language and Communication," (produced by the Moody Institute of Science, Santa Monica Blvd., W. Los Angeles, Cal. 11428), based on the development of the history of language. Discuss the various ways man has learned to communicate with others, such as sign language, drawings, symbols and gestures.

8mm Film Loop Activity   Short, single-loop 8mm concept films are ideal for creative writing periods, individualized language experience and for providing information for research and class discussion periods. A film loop on an historic event, science experiment or nature study, makes ideal fodder for oral and written exercises.

DRAMATIZATION

The Importance of Dramatics in Language

All pupils have some degree of creativity within them, and it is important that the classroom teacher encourage pupils to participate in diversified kinds of activities and be given full opportunities for expression. Creative dramatics helps the child understand himself and others. This is particularly true when role-playing techniques are utilized. In addition, dramatics fosters confidence and poise and helps children fully develop skills in observation, imagination, speaking and listening.

Vicarious Primary Experiences

At the primary level, dramatic plays may be based on familiar experiences, such has playing house, playing school or acting out a favorite story. When children reach the intermediate level of dramatization, dramatic plays and socio-drama emerge from all subject areas, reading, social studies and music, as well as from personal experience.

Familiar Pantomime Activities for Primary Pupils

The least complex form of creative expression is pantomime. Children can learn the art of pantomime readily from watching motion pictures and television. Beginning pantomime activities should allow pupils to work individually as well as in groups. They may re-enact such common-place and familiar activities as eating their breakfast, walking through a supermarket and selecting groceries, or picking and smelling flowers.

Informal Dramatics Activities

Too often we teachers associate costumes and elaborate scenery with the success of dramatic presentations. However, putting on a creative, informal drama can be just as productive for children. Allow the children to take a story, song or poem as a point of departure, and dramatize their own ideas in their own words. A dramatization without props or costumes calls for the highest degree of imagination—which children have!

Socio-Drama in the Language Arts Program

One area of oral expression often neglected is the socio-drama. Socio-dramas can be a wonderful outlet in a child's expression of feelings and attitudes. A socio-drama also allows a child to share a pleasant or un-pleasant experience with his classmates. As in pantomime, such a drama may be performed by an individual or group. In socio-dramas, the teacher can guide pupils in dramatizing an incident that *has* happened, as well as enacting what *might* have happened.

Socio-Drama and Puppetry

Socio-drama, through puppetry, is a most appealing technique in English for exploring appropriate social behavior. The teacher can direct students in activities with puppets that involve family relationships and by developing informal playlets that demonstrate everyday patterns of behavior and recreate natural conversations.

Tableaux Teach Stage Presence

In turning our attention to formal dramatics, let's not overlook *tableaux,* which give pupils the feeling of stage presence without the pressures of memorizing lines. In dramatizations, whether for classroom or assembly, the emphasis of presentation should be a combination of ready-made plays, but we should foster motivation in our students to create plays of their own. To accomplish this objective, read simple one-act plays to the class and encourage discussion of the play's meaning and characters. One imaginative teacher in Arlington, Virginia, initiated a discussion of colors and the way colors make pupils feel.

Sources of Ideas for Assemblies

Teachers have mixed emotions about assembly programs. Perhaps the biggest problem is finding a source of ideas for assembly programs. Two reliable publications, *The Instructor* and *Grade Teacher,* which are geared for the elementary school teacher, usually contain excellent articles as regular features on assemblies as well as teacher solicited ideas. Another excellent source is *Producing Successful School Assembly Programs,* published as part of the Prentice-Hall Education Series.

Class Meetings

Meetings, whether in the form of a club or committee, are another excellent device for encouraging positive language arts contributions. Throughout this exercise children can be directed in the steps of conducting a meeting along modified rules of parliamentary procedure. Children, when exposed to this oral outlet, will discover the value of having rules for conducting meetings, as well as learn respect for the rights of others to express their opinions. All elements of parliamentary procedure should be provided.

Dynamic Debating

Debate is a dynamic form of oral expression. A good debater has to be not only a good speaker and listener, but a thinker as well. The topic selected for discussion must be one in which there is more than one side to the issue. A study of famous historical debates is a good starting place for exposing children to a most challenging auditory language arts activity. Debates taped from suitable public affairs programs will give the children a pattern or format to follow.

Round Table and Panel Discussions

Round table and panel discussions can be stimulating oral experiences. Round table discussion is ideal for small group conferences. Using this technique of discussing problems, the teacher should appoint as chairman an able pupil who will supply opening questions, keep the discussion from straying and have the ability to summarize. The panel discussion is much like a round table, but it is usually presented before a class or assembly audience. Successful panel discussions are limited to three or four members, are informal, and each of the members has engaged in thoughtful research.

Relaxing Pupils for Oral Participation Activities

Oral skills and preparation do not have to be elaborate for individually prepared talks, oral readings, or oral book reports. The teacher, however, must make pupils cognizant that they must make extensive preparation, which includes correct pronunciation practice in speaking in a clear, pleasant voice. Shy speakers can be encouraged to practice before small groups of classmates so that they will become free and relaxed in their presentations.

PRIMARY ACTIVITIES

Mystery Box Use the element of mystery to encourage oral and sensory responses. Place a series of objects of varied textures in an opened carton into which children can reach and touch the objects, feel them and describe the materials they are feeling. Later, have the class make up a list of words that describe the textures. A variation of this activity is placing sound-producing objects in the box.

Action Poems Assign each child a poem in which the actions can be pantomimed or acted out; for example, Robert Louis Stevenson's "Time to Rise" or perhaps a weather poem. Selections like "Weather Vane," from *Action Songs* by Helen J. Fletcher (distributed by Teachers Publishing Company, Darien, Connecticut 06820), "The Owl and the Pussy-Cat" and other samples, would be ideal for such poetry.

Let's Pretend An interesting, informal, and creative dramatic activity is to have each child make a wand, simple crown or witch's hat from construction paper or oaktag, covered with any shiny-surfaced wrapping paper. Use these props for a playlet or pantomime fairyland story with a Good Fairy and Wicked Witch. One child, acting as a Wizard in this impromptu activity, may pretend that he has changed other children into enchanted animals, insects or colorful Mother Goose people.

Rock Beings Use rocks no larger than three to four inches and, by utilizing colored adhesive tape and glued buttons, make up imaginative rock people. Plan to use these rock people to initiate lively discussions on the visual impression left by each rock creature.

INTERMEDIATE ACTIVITIES

Punctuation and Capitalization Pass out printed word and punctuation cards for each child. These cards will have the markings of what children already know in written language or learning at the time. The teacher reads aloud a sentence and each child who holds the same word or punctuation that will fit the sentence, moves to the front of the room and arranges himself, with his word in the correct sequence. Later, have the students substitute sound and actions for words and punctuation. Another variation of this, which should appeal to the imagination of children, is to have them interpret the words and punctuation marks, each child telling the others about his word.

Malapropisms In the annals of theatrical history there never has been a more colorful and humorous character than Mrs. Malaprop, created by the eighteenth century playwright Richard Brimsly Sheridan in his play *The Rivals*. As you may remember, Mrs. Malaprop, who was a chronic word mis-user and abuser, would thoughtlessly blurt out such inappropriate words or expressions as, "Lead the way, we'll *proceed.*" Such a word, improperly used, is termed a *malapropism*. Have class committees make a series of their own malapropisms and ask the rest of the class to analyze and correct these mixed up expressions.

What's My Line? One of the finer television panel programs has been "What's My Line?" An imaginative activity, based on this program, is to have committees do extensive research on some interesting occupation or famous person. Then, with one student assuming the role, have a panel of four students try to guess the occupation or identity of the person.

Listening to Compare Differences in Reporting There is quite a difference between merely hearing as contrasted to seeing *and* hearing. Tell the class to study news events or a sportscast, first on the radio, then the same event on television. A lively discussion on the two forms of reporting can touch upon the methods of reporting, accuracy of the accounts, choice of vocabulary words and the amount of information gained through each media.

Baby Talk Spend several sessions with children in which you may base a discussion on how a child's speech, from early babbling baby talk through ages three to five, develops through to teen and adult age.

Syllabication Show children how syllabication makes a difference in how a word is pronounced. List on the chalkboard a series of words syllabized with only one choice of those correctly stated. Ask children to pronounce each of the selections.

SUMMARY

Utilization of the tape recorder can certainly be justified in the language arts curriculum, especially in all aspects of oral expression, be they dramatics, speech making, oral reports or class discussions. As in reading, radio and records serve as a model for good language patterns and as stimulation for better written language.

As has been previously noted, graphics, with its multi-faceted variations, can motivate and clarify ideas and help pupils interpret information relative to written and oral language pursuits. One of the most tedious tasks with which teachers are confronted is the correcting of pupil compositions and related written exercises. Using the opaque or overhead projector not only facilitates the correction procedure, but what is more important, makes it a meaningful educational experience for the students.

The imaginative teacher will find filmstrips to be an excellent stimulant for divergent forms of oral and written expression. Motion pictures, whether 16mm, 8mm or film loops, can lead to a fascinating excursion into creative language exercises and will serve as an attractive device for teaching such key skills as outlining and paragraphing.

Are teachers utilizing dramatics experiences with the proper touch of ingenuity in the language arts program? If the answer is an unadulterated *no,* it is hoped that the teacher will give more thought to this particular visual technique in order to evolve a more appealing instructional program for their pupils in Language Arts.

4

BETTER SPELLING
THROUGH
AUDIO-VISUAL INSTRUCTION

There is nothing more jarring to the reader of a book, or even a simple letter, than to come across an obviously misspelled word. The necessity of instilling good spelling habits in language arts must begin early, at the primary level. Certainly, the foundation of positive spelling patterns is a prime function of the classroom instructor. Children must be convinced of the need for developing good spelling practices. And the importance of these skills, in a sense, demands that the teacher establish a program that elicits from children special interest in spelling. The judicious use of audio-visual aids and creative teaching techniques can accomplish such laudable objectives.

Increase the morale of your class by teaching spelling by tape. Fine, useful commercially-produced and taped spelling lessons are available, but the best are spelling tapes prepared by the classroom teacher. Such tapes are ideal for individual spelling instruction and remedial work, review and for drill and test purposes. The spoken rhetoric of radio and records can help pupils compare and differentiate between how a word sounds and the way it is spelled.

The traditional methodology of spelling usually calls for mastery of weekly spelling words and definitions. The chalkboard, when used for spelling games, instills a healthy spirit of competition, and, above all, invests the subject with variety and an aura of imagination which will enhance the entire spelling program.

Sometimes bulletin boards, both as vehicles for teaching effective spelling habits and as reinforcement devices, are neglected. Social studies and science are often looked upon as more favored subjects for bulletin board displays. For this reason, the spirit of competition and challenge is a basic ingredient for effective spelling displays.

Motion pictures have been with us for over half a century, and there can be no doubt television is here to stay. The teacher should adapt these dynamic audio-visual media to his educational ends in order to develop more proficient spelling.

TAPE TECHNIQUES IN SPELLING

Tapes to Listen by

Perhaps the prime value of the tape recorder in spelling is that it makes pupils more alert and attentive. If they don't listen the first time around, they won't get it at all.

Better Listening Equals Better Spelling

Tape recordings of spelling words for test or drill purposes help increase the pupil's ability to listen and concentrate more fully, and above all, save the classroom teacher precious time. This technique allows the teacher to be a participant in taping the exercise, for the classroom teacher, in making his own tapes, will, by necessity, become conscious of his pronunciation, tone of voice and rate of speed.

The Role of Phonics in Spelling

Tapes may not only be made of words themselves, but, in addition, recitations of key spelling rules may also be recorded. Tapes should also verbally remind pupils that a portion of our words are not spelled phonetically and do not necessarily follow the rules.

The Burlington Technique

A technique used successfully in the Burlington, Massachusetts schools is presenting one spelling rule or sound at a time, in carefully paced steps. A good recording of this nature will repeat the spelling rule several times, besides giving oral applications and exceptions to the rule. Dittoed worksheets are used to reinforce and supplement the rules.

Correlation to Spelling Texts and Workbooks

A library of spelling tapes, patterned on any spelling program (including the new Botel spelling linguistic approach), is valuable for individualized instruction, and allows the pupil to make up missed work and progress in spelling at his own rate.

Spelling Tape Libraries

Schools in Mineola, New York, and Norwalk, Connecticut, have made extensive spelling tape libraries based on approved basal spelling texts. In these schools spelling by tape is accomplished by utilizing listening centers or individual carrels, either in the classroom or in the library. Taped lessons are labeled according to grade level and lesson, and under this program, each child is free to progress at his own rate.

Tape as Drillmaster

Why not use the tape recorder as a word drillmaster? The first step in this procedure is to compile a list of spelling words and tape them. Limit them to a maximum of twenty words. Use a dittoed list as a supplement to the taped lesson so that the pupil can refer to the written word when he hears it on the tape. As extra drill, spell the words at random, and have the child see if he can pronounce the words aloud. Either the teacher or a pupil committee can prepare one list of words spelled the way they sound and another list of the completely un-phonetical. For example, a teacher could tape a series of words, such as ocean ('o shən), dozen ('dəz n), gnaw ('nô) fierce ('fi(ə)rs), patience ('pā shən(t)s), which are *not* spelled the way they sound, and contrast them with words which are fundamentally phonetic, such as rag, forgot, pit, go and sung. These taped lists are conducive to stimulating spelling lessons and language sessions.

TAPE ACTIVITIES FOR ALL LEVELS

Pupil Puzzlers Have pupils make up spelling puzzles, riddles or poems based on spelling rules; then record them on tape.

Spelling Detective Teacher and student, being careful not to be too specific, could give aural clues on tape about appropriate spelling words. The main idea is to have someone in the class identify the word and spell it correctly.

Taped Conversations Ask class committees to record a list of words they hear on radio and records or those heard in conversations. While these tapes are being played, have the rest of the class use dictionaries as a check on the pronunciation and meaning of the words.

BULLETIN BOARD

Multi-Purpose Bulletin Board Display

Teachers, for years, have used the classroom bulletin board almost exclusively as a means to reward achievement in spelling by placing the 100 percent papers on display. Certainly, this reliable visual aid can be put to a more meaningful use, by the inventive classroom teacher, to motivate and sustain interest in spelling and to promote good spelling habits. As in other subject matter areas, the spelling bulletin board can be employed for the purpose of review and enrichment. Bulletin boards can also foster interest in spelling by the simple means of puzzles, tongue twisters and riddles.

Dramatic Effects with Spelling

"It pays to advertise" is the often repeated slogan of Madison Avenue. Similarly, new spelling words can be dramatically advertised with the employment of printed words accompanied by carefully selected and appealing magazine illustrations and drawings displayed on bulletin boards. Spelling is more meaningful if the words are used in a *visual* context rather than in an *audio* context.

Spelling bulletin boards will also be more effective if pupils are encouraged to become actively involved in their planning and maintenance. Teachers should attempt to make sure spelling bulletin boards are flexible, and that they do not become outdated.

Functional Spelling Bulletin Boards

Functional spelling bulletin boards should focus attention on some key spelling rules, the role of syllabication, and dictionary skills. Spelling bulletin boards must make pupils cognizant of the fact that not all words are phonetic, and that not all words follow rules (Figure 4-1).

PRIMARY BULLETIN BOARD ACTIVITIES

Outer Space   A departure from the traditional weekly display of the best of pupils' spelling papers is to ask each pupil to print his name on a colorful construction paper, rocket cutout, and place it against a science background suggestive of outer space and the solar system. Any student having a perfect paper could visually penetrate beyond the earth's atmosphere. Pupils missing a few words might only move outward to the

Photo taken by author

Figure 4-1
Word Families Bulletin Board Photo

stratosphere or ionosphere. A poor spelling paper might confine a pupil's rocket cutout to the lower atmosphere and an extremely poor speller could be grounded until he improves.

Homonymizing Phonics and Homophone Cutouts An excellent way to demonstrate groups of similarly sounding words is to plan a bulletin board where like-sounding words are printed on duplicate shapes of animals and objects, such as rabbits, bears or apples. These cutouts serve to remind students that, although words are pronounced the same, they can have different meanings and spelling.

Don't Fall Overboard! Place on the bulletin board something simulating the ocean, or body of water with boats on it. Cutout boats are placed on the bulletin board ocean. Simple cutout people, representing successful spellers, can climb aboard or safely stand in the boat. Any pupil who fails to achieve a satisfactory grade in a spelling test, or does poorly in an oral spelldown, will fall in the briny brink.

INTERMEDIATE BULLETIN BOARD ACTIVITIES

Illustrate the Word   Give each pupil a spelling word from the current word list, and ask him to make a simple drawing of the word on 8½ x 11″ paper. Place the completed colored drawing on the bulletin board. Request that pupils *not* spell out the word on the drawing; in fact, leave a blank space on the drawing at the bottom of the paper, and ask the rest of the class to guess the identity of the word depicted in the drawing. When someone correctly identifies the word and can spell it correctly, allow the pupil to fill in the word in the blank space provided.

Tongue Twisters and Silly Sentences   Ask pupils to compose riddles, silly sentences or tongue twisters with a key spelling word in it. Select the best riddles, silly sentences and tongue twisters, and print them on oaktag or plain white paper with a felt marker. This type of spelling bulletin board could become a regular feature of weekly spelling lessons.

Spelling Doctor   Children, like adults, enjoy a good mystery. Using this as motivation, place a group of misspelled "mystery" words on colored construction paper on the bulletin board. Ask pupils to play detective to determine what the spelling error is, and give the correct spelling of each word. A variation of this is to play "spelling doctor" in which pupils act as "spelling practitioner" and diagnose what the problem or error is in each spelling word (Figure 4-2).

Illustration by Mary Farrell

Figure 4-2
Spelling Doctor

Words in Other Languages   Take a common Anglo-Saxon spelling word and prepare a bulletin board display which compares this English word with the spelling and pronunciation of the word in other languages. For example, the number "one" is "uno" in Spanish. Foreign spelling forms, when supplemented with appropriate drawings and graphics printed on oaktag, enable pupils to develop key visual and auditory skills in spelling.

CHALKBOARD TECHNIQUES

The Old Reliable

The chalkboard still remains as a sturdy mainstay in spelling instruction, undaunted and not visibly intimidated by some of our newer audio-visual equipment.

Idea Games and Functional Instruction

It is perhaps in the area of spelling games, such as the traditional "hangman" and spelling baseball games, that the chalkboard has its greatest value—besides its normal employment as a main vehicle for recording words, analyzing, drilling, word structure and writing down rules.

Chalkboard Demands Attention

The teacher at the chalkboard commands everyone's attention. Using colored chalk will intensify their interest. The chalkboard in spelling permits the pupil to easily become an active participant in the lesson.

PRIMARY CHALKBOARD ACTIVITIES

Supply the Missing Word   Write on the chalkboard a series of interesting sentences which omit a key spelling word that the pupils must supply.

Spell It with Music   Several primary classroom teachers have successfully combined spelling with musical knowledge. Draw on the chalkboard a series of musical staffs with notes. The notes, when shown in order, readily spell out simple words like go, den, get or bag.

Don't Wreck the Train!   On the chalkboard prepare a sketch of a simple train, with a series of boxes to represent cars. The teacher or a pupil can select a spelling word from the assigned list and say it orally, giving the class clues to the number of letters in the word. Then ask other pupils to place one letter at a time in one correct space at a time. If an incorrect letter is put in the box, the train is derailed. In order to get the train repaired and back on the right track, other pupils must come up with the right letter in the correct place. The spelling train reaches its destination only after all words are correctly placed (Figure 4-3).

INTERMEDIATE CHALKBOARD ACTIVITIES

Rhyme All the Time Place spelling words on the chalkboard and direct pupils to find other words that rhyme harmoniously with those on the board. To expand the activity, pupils can be directed to other language arts areas and reading for good samples of poetry. Encourage pupils to use the dictionary and thesaurus to check on pronunciation and match rhyming words.

The Spelling Enrichment Time Teacher and pupil committees can compile lists of words from other subject areas and list them on slips of paper which may be put in a box. These words are later distributed to the class. Dictionaries should be available for easy reference. Have pupils write the words they have drawn from the box on the chalkboard, and see if they know the meaning of the words. If the pupil who has the word doesn't know its meaning, he can ask his classmates to check on it in the dictionary. By writing each word on the chalkboard, fellow pupils

Illustration by Mary Farrell

Figure 4-3
Don't Wreck the Train!

are able to evolve an expansive spelling list and learn the meaning or key words in various subject areas.

Scrambled Letters Place on the chalkboard a series of words with the letters scrambled and select individual pupils to unscramble the letters so that the word is formed correctly.

Chalkboard Scrabble Write on the chalkboard a series of root words of two to three syllables, and have children derive other words from the root words on the board. The teacher can precede this activity with a lesson on structural relationships, showing word forms such as safe, safety, safely, or kind, kindly, kindness.

MOTION PICTURES AND TELEVISION

The Dominant Audio-Visual Media

The children of this generation are certainly influenced by two of our most powerful audio-visual forces, motion pictures and television, which are an integral part of today's environment. Why not harness these potent sight and sound media for effective learning in spelling instruction and enrichment purposes?

Increase Your Spelling Vocabulary

With both television and films, children are exposed to numerous examples of sight and sound vocabulary. Words are more meaningful via these media in spelling because they can be presented in a visual context with the benefit of imaginative and attractive settings.

Source of Pupil Games

Films and television can be the basis of a variety of spelling games. Panel and quiz programs make an ideal nucleus of ideas for spelling enrichment activities.

Dramatics and Spelling

Children and teachers alike, after watching motion pictures and television, can use numerous observations of these media as a source of vicarious experience in dramatic exercises for informal playlets, pantomime, shadow plays and puppetry, which in turn, they can use to act out spelling words.

Pantomime Quiz Write on slips of paper a list of spelling words, distribute them to small groups of pupils, and ask them to make up pantomime playlets. The rest of the class has to guess the identity of the spelling words being dramatized visually. A variation is the old-fashioned charades.

Vocabulary Confusion   Some words have multiple meanings. With motion pictures, a teacher can preview a film and jot down a list of words that have several meanings. After showing the particular film to the class, ask the pupils to discuss how these terms were used in the films. Films and television can also be used as an audio-visual frame of reference to clarify meanings of many words.

Puppetry Spelling Bee   Add spice and variety to the old-fashioned spelling bee by using puppets manipulated by students to spell out the words. Shy spellers, at the primary level, will like puppets as stand-ins for themselves.

Password   Another popular quiz program can serve as the basis for a pleasurable spelling activity. The game is played with two teams, each team consisting of two members. A pupil or teacher-moderator writes a spelling word on a 3 x 5" card or slip of paper and hands it to one of the members of the team. The other co-partner must guess the identity of the word. One-word clues are given by a helping partner, usually by suggesting synonyms or word association phrases, until the partner guesses the word or gives up. As in the TV program, time limits can be set for answering and a point system can be worked out for correct responses.

SUMMARY

There are an increasing number of companies that produce spelling tapes based on basal spelling series. While these ready-made tapes are most welcome, teachers, if they have ample time, may tape lessons of their own. In addition, tape recorders can be a catylyst for exercises in auditory discrimination and enrichment activities.

Sometimes in the glittering array of newer audio-visual devices, we as teachers may lose sight of the still valuable chalkboard and bulletin board. All that these old standbys need is a slight seasoning of imagination by both pupils and teacher.

As noted, the influence of motion pictures and television should not be denied. It is up to the teacher to utilize these media in constructive and imaginative ways to produce better and more effective spellers.

5

AUDIO-VISUAL METHODS FOR TEACHING PENMANSHIP

Handwriting is a paradoxical subject. There seems to be a revival of interest in good handwriting practice as indicated by the ever-increasing number of articles in educational journals on this key subject skill area. Yet, is interest alone sufficient? Many critics of today's handwriting instruction contend that the majority of teachers are not trained to teach this vital skill effectively. If this reasoning is correct, we then should plan to aid teachers, at the same time that we interest pupils, and incorporate and increase the frequency of the use of visual aids in handwriting instruction.

In devising successful techniques and activities with visual material certain characteristics of good handwriting programs must be recognized. First, a penmanship readiness program should start in kindergarten, where children are given exercises to develop eye-hand coordination. This can best be achieved by such activities as painting, drawing, doing puzzles, sewing, chalk drawing and playing with blocks.

Handwriting is a skill learned primarily via visual means. Visual aids at all levels are utilized, beginning in the lower grades where *manuscript* is taught up to the third grade and continuing through the change-over to cursive penmanship. The stress in fundamentals in penmanship during the formative handwriting years is on proper posture, hand position, correct letter formation, alignment, spacing and uniform slant.

At the intermediate level, the classroom teacher is responsible for maintaining and further strengthening positive writing habits, and correcting any faulty handwriting problems that pupils have developed. Another key function of all teachers, especially at this level, is to provide

motivation and encouragement to pupils so that each is inspired to take pride in his handwriting.

At the upper grades the main criteria for handwriting evaluation are legibility and neatness. Certainly, we strive for a certain positive uniformity or set of standards in handwriting; yet, recognition of individuality is a necessity in instruction in each pupil's handwriting. Cognizance of this must be an integral feature in a teacher's planning in this vital skill area. It is almost impossible to get each pupil to write perfectly; as with fingerprints, no two people have exactly the same type of handwriting. While we desire distinctiveness in handwriting, we must still insist on quality of readability and neatness in handwriting. Legibility has most certainly a strong correlation to spelling and written language. Poorly formed t's and d's, e's that look like i's, and other careless writing habits can subtract from a pupil's overall achievement in these subject areas.

AUDIO-VISUAL TECHNIQUES

Teaching Handwriting by Audio Means

Although penmanship is taught primarily through visual techniques and materials, there are certain audio techniques and devices, such as the tape recorder and disc recording, that can be effectively employed for instruction in this skill.

Say It with Records

Rhythmic chants recorded on tape may represent audio symbols or cues for straight lines, slant strokes and curves or circles, as pupils practice these handwriting formations in order to develop better neuromuscular maturity. Max Rosenhaus of Zaner-Bloser Company (612 North Park St., Columbus, Ohio 43215) has employed the rhythm of music to teach strokes and other handwriting patterns. Soft mood music can also provide a pleasant working atmosphere for penmanship practice.

Chalkboard of Visual Handwriting Models

Imitation is one of the sincerest forms of flattery. Imitation of good handwriting forms and proper posture are not to be frowned upon. Imaginative bulletin board displays, simple stick figure drawings and charts drawn with a felt pen, good posture poses or samples of good printing and writing, forms cut from old magazines, all are excellent sources of functional visuals. Of course, samples of good handwriting done by pupils should always be prominently displayed.

Handwriting Readiness

Skywriting, or writing in the air, gives pupils experience in practicing various letter formations. This prewriting or skywriting experience should precede handwriting drill, either on the chalkboard or on paper at the pupil's desk.

Availability of Handwriting Aids

Handwriting manuals and packaged commercial programs have been available for years, including a variety of handwriting aids which show step-by-step good systematic letter formation and proper handwriting posture.

Handwriting Analysis and Instruction

The opaque and overhead projector are extremely valuable in teaching handwriting skills. Samples of pupils' handwriting can be placed on the opaque for instant analysis. Teachers can have pupils practice their handwriting on the overhead by writing directly with a grease pencil on a roll of acetate. Commercial acetates of good penmanship formation are available and can also be made by the teacher or pupils from their own work.

Chalkboard Handwriting Instruction Mainstay

The teacher's hand and ever reliable chalkboard are still the classroom teacher's top visual aids. As with the bulletin board, teachers can sketch simple line drawings or skeleton figures on the chalkboard in order to demonstrate correct body position for pupils. Conventional wall alphabets of *manuscript* and cursive writing should always be on display above the chalkboard.

Handwriting Ditto Masters Program

One interesting and effective visual handwriting aid is made available by W. A. Sheaffer Pen Company, Fort Madison, Iowa, in the form of a ditto master kit, "Handwriting Practice 3-6" which covers all aspects of cursive handwriting. Particularly helpful is the slant chart, made from a ditto master, which may be slipped under the pupil's practice paper. The chart shows through the paper and guides the pupil towards proper slant. Of course, homemade slant guides can be made with a felt pen on cardboard which will achieve the same purpose.

The W. A. Scheaffer Pen Company ditto masters were not intended to be utilized as ends in themselves, but were to be used as a means for providing material for pupil participation and practice. As in any subject area, ditto material must be supplemented by actual teacher instruction and the selective incorporation of such visuals as the chalkboard, transparencies and filmstrips to demonstrate graphically the proper letter formation, alignment and spacing skills so necessary for good handwriting.

Peterson Colorgraph Handwriting System

Another interesting commercial program is the Colorgraph Method. This system breaks letter forms into specific basic writing strokes using color for effective visual discrimination. The program has a complete range of materials for handwriting, including posture charts, slant reminders and grading scales. This may be secured from Peterson "Directed Handwriting," Greensburg, Pennsylvania, 15602.

Concept Visualizer System

The Concept Visualizer handwriting program offers both horizontal and vertical, manuscript and cursive penmanship charts, and pupil handwriting guide pads. One novel feature of this program is the employment of transparent acetate used in connection with the aforementioned pupil handwriting practice pads. The acetate, if first used for demonstration purposes on the overhead projector, can later be placed over a pupil's work in order to check accuracy of letter formation (the transparent acetate sheets easily fit children's work size of ½″ ruled paper). For information, contact Concept Visualizer at 609 W. 51st Street, New York, N.Y. 10019.

Wearever Handwriting Kits

The Wearever handwriting kits are free and include a teacher's manual, pupil handwriting certificates and writing test blanks. Write to David Kahn, Inc. (Wearever Pen), North Bergen, New Jersey.

HANDWRITING ENRICHMENT ACTIVITIES

History of Writing Encourage pupil research on various forms of writing and printing from earliest times or compare printed and written penmanship symbols from people of other countries. Prepare a bulletin board display based on this theme. Pupil-made charts or drawings and magazine cutout illustrations may be supplemented by compositions and research papers based on the history of writing.

Handwriting Posture   Ask the class to collect newspaper and magazine pictures demonstrating good handwriting positions. To show contrast, collect pictures of people with poor posture.

Tracing Letters   Employ the opaque projector to project words on the chalkboard and assign two or three children, depending on space, to go to the chalkboard and trace the words. Students may copy the words traced and check them with the originals. They may also outline the letters, if needed, as was done with the skywriting technique.

Outline a Pupil's Letter   Place a series of dot outlines of different letters either on a ditto or mimeograph, or place a series of these outlines on the chalkboard. Then have a child connect the dots in order to trace the correct letter form.

Guess Whose Handwriting   Since every person's handwriting is unique, put the spotlight on the distinctive features and style of every pupil's handwriting. Ask your group of pupils to write short paragraphs which are placed on the opaque projector without their names showing. Ask the rest of the class to play detective and identify the writing of the other children. It is important that the teacher guide students in analyzing the handwriting samples they are viewing in a constructive fashion.

Handwriting Folder   After the class has been shown good samples of handwriting by means of such visual aids as the chalkboard, opaque and overhead projector, let them practice handwriting and place samples of their work, which are dated, in a special penmanship folder. From time to time ask pupils to compare previous samples of their writing to the results of later visual instruction sessions and handwriting samples.

Handwriting Caricatures   While it will not teach good penmanship form, this imaginative handwriting activity will heighten interest in handwriting. Take a printed or manuscript letter like an A or B, and encourage pupils to make an amusing caricature of it, with the art teacher's assistance. For example, the letter can serve as the basis for caricatures for a "b" word like boy, bugs, etc.

SUMMARY

Certainly, legibility in penmanship is one of the most desirous skills in our elementary school curriculum. Ease of writing and individual style must be considered. A successful handwriting program encompasses pre-writing experiences, such as sky-writing, neuromuscular ability, reading ability, and the pupil's interest in good writing.

More and more, the extensive and intelligent use of visual aids can do much to help resolve handwriting difficulties and enhance the overall quality of penmanship. Any visual aid, whether a good commercially-prepared one from a reliable company or a home-made device, is a prime necessity for a truly stimulating and imaginative handwriting program.

6

MORE EFFECTIVE MATH INSTRUCTION USING AUDIO-VISUAL MATERIALS

Mathematics certainly should be every bit as exciting a subject as reading, science and social studies. Whether simple or complex, audio-visual materials, when wisely employed, help make mathematics more readily understandable and imbue the subject with attractiveness that engages the interest of each pupil, whether he is a slow, average or fast learner.

The tape recorder serves mathematics best as an appealing drillmaster, reviewer or reinforcer. With imagination and ingenuity, mathematics drill can become something a pupil can look forward to, rather than dread.

The overhead projector is really coming into its own in the field of elementary mathematics instruction. Some people believe the overhead should replace the chalkboard completely. This it should never do, but it has undoubtedly a wider degree of flexibility in mathematics than the chalkboard.

For countless years, the classroom bulletin board has been an indispensable asset to the mathematics teacher. Today it still remains as valuable. Without question, a creative bulletin board, with brain teasers and puzzles, supplies students with the opportunity to think independently and breathe the spirit of challenge into a subject that can fall into a pattern of drudgery and repetitiousness.

Mathematics, like science, will take on greater meaning if teachers will incorporate, as part and parcel of their teaching, the judicious and creative use of models, realia and displays.

Filmstrips and slides can enhance the mathematics program if they are used intelligently; otherwise, their effectiveness is weakened. Most important, filmstrips and slides should augment and illustrate a lesson, but they should never serve as ends in themselves. Their prime role in instruction is to supplement and review mathematics.

TAPE RECORDER

Tapes for Basic Math and Mental Arithmetic Drill

Whether teachers are utilizing today's modern mathematics or traditional arithmetic, drill on certain basics in mathematics has always been a necessity in the program. Put some zip into old-fashioned drill by using the tape recorder. Tape recordings may be used to teach basic facts for the entire class or to give individual review for additional drill.

Taped lessons have the advantage of helping emancipate pupils from complete reliance on paper and pencil. Specifically, they enable pupils to develop better listening skills in mathematics, increase speed, and most important, help students develop proficiency in mental computation.

Experienced teachers have found taped drills in arithmetic operations should run four to five minutes for the questions and one or two minutes for pupil responses. Naturally, problem solving tapes, depending on the degree of difficulty, will necessitate more time.

Math Sharing Program and Tape Library

Teachers, for years, have used the chalkboard or dittoed masters for test purposes. The tape recorder can gainfully be utilized for this express purpose. One obvious advantage in employing these tapes is to build up an indexed, taped mathematics library and lesson tape exchange. Your fellow teachers may want to set up a sharing program.

Comprehensive Tape Library

In compiling a mathematics tape library that will include lessons, drills and tests, it is important to store them carefully in a readily accessible place. In addition, a written file on 3 x 5" index cards, with short descriptions of the contents of tapes, will make it easier for the classroom teacher to utilize them in planning lessons with continuity.

PRIMARY TAPE ACTIVITIES

Pupil Participation Tapes The element of student participation should be considered in mathematics tapes for the primary level. Allow and encourage children to contribute their own simple mathematics questions or problems for taping.

Tell Me a Math Story Teachers, particularly at the primary level, should have pupils make up stories which involve an interesting arithmetic problem; also they should make up a series of mathematics riddles which the class can try to identify or solve.

Telling Time Construct a homemade clock or utilize a commercial clock face with a pair of movable hands. Use audio tapes of clocks playing the appropriate number of chimes for the respective hours, and simultaneously have pupils place the hands in the correct position. This creates a visual step beyond the strictly aural, primary pupil participation tapes.

INTERMEDIATE TAPE ACTIVITIES

Taped Math Contest Assign committees of pupils to make up a series of mathematics problems which will be utilized to stimulate what might be called a mathematics question and answer bee, an activity in which the class may be divided into two sides. Or as added competition, a contest can be held with pupils in other classes at the same grade level. Certainly the spirit of challenge and competition posed by audio puzzles can be a dynamic ingredient in mathematics.

Beat the Tape Math Game Prepare tapes in which certain mathematical combinations and problems are posed and which, after a pause, the tape narrator divulges answers. Individual pupils try to give the correct answer before the tape does. The taped question and answer sessions may be accelerated, depending on the ability of the group.

OVERHEAD PROJECTOR TECHNIQUES

The overhead projector can be a dynamic asset to the teacher of mathematics. Teacher-prepared or commercially-made transparencies can be saved and re-used from year to year. Where commercial transparencies are unavailable, teachers can prepare difficult mathematics exercises and diagrams which may, in some instances, better meet the needs of students.

Opaque Materials for Overhead Math Instruction

The overhead makes mathematics less abstract and more meaningful. On the stage of the overhead, opaque objects like checkers, coins or buttons enable the teacher to illustrate the concept of *sets*. Opaque cutouts of geometric shapes, projected on the overhead, foster interest in this subject area. Likewise, transparent rulers and protractors may be used in the instruction of linear measurement, as well as to demonstrate measuring angles.

As is the case in many other subjects, mathematics assignments and homework may be projected on a screen. Many creative teachers are using inexpensive substitute acetates on reprocessed X-ray plates. Pupils may do their homework on these inexpensive acetates. The teacher, when projecting a pupil's work for correction, should mask out the student's name on the transparency, to preserve anonymity.

Instruction with Graphs, Charts and Business Forms

The overhead projector is also an excellent aid in teaching bar and line graphs; the interest of pupils may be aroused by having them plot graphs and charts. Transparencies made of simple sales and business forms, such as checks, may be used as a device to make basic arithmetic operations and procedures more meaningful (Figure 6-1).

Courtesy of Elwood Board of Education, N.Y.

Figure 6-1

Teaching Math Fundamentals with the Overhead

Use of Animation in Math Instruction

Without certain touches of realistic "cartoon" humor mathematics can be a deadly subject to many children. A teacher can incorporate into transparencies the element of animation to demonstrate key mathematical rules. Morton Schultz, in his book "The Teacher and Overhead Projection," goes into this technique in great detail.

The teacher- or pupil-made transparency is an ideal way to teach fractions. Students can be asked to make illustrations on transparencies to demonstrate their knowledge of fractional principles. Opaque cutouts of fractional parts may be effectively employed in teaching this mathematical concept (Figure 6-2).

Courtesy of Charles Beseler Company, East Orange, N.J.

Figure 6-2

Fractions Are Easy

Geometric Manipulative Devices

Teacher-made manipulative devices to introduce geometric shapes can be constructed of oaktag and hinged together with paper fasteners or pin clips. By movement of the parts of the device, the teacher and pupil can readily change its shape on the stage of the overhead.

PRIMARY OVERHEAD ACTIVITIES

"Math Bingo"   Make opaque cutouts patterned after various geometric shapes to show to the class. Next, distribute handmade mathematics bingo cards with drawn geometric shapes similar to the corresponding shapes to be shown later, the idea being to match the opaque-held cutouts with the pupils' geometric-patterned bingo cards.

Let's Play Teacher   Children love to imitate adults, including such a role as teacher. Before the conclusion of a mathematics unit, ask for pupil volunteers to present a simple mathematics lesson of their own where they may use the overhead and transparency to review and reinforce specific mathematical concepts.

INTERMEDIATE OVERHEAD ACTIVITIES

Math Crossword Puzzles   Encourage pupils to prepare mathematical crossword puzzle transparencies. Discarded or old mathematics workbooks and textbooks could be used as sources of each puzzle. Supplemental dittoed masters of some puzzles will enhance the lesson immeasurably.

Mystery Math   Either the teacher or pupils can make up mathematics riddles or stories involving mathematical principles or operations. The answers to the riddles or stories could be masked out with opaque material or be placed on overlays.

BULLETIN BOARD

The Ever-Reliable Bulletin Board

The bulletin board, along with the chalkboard and more recently, the overhead projector, are probably the most important and reliable visual devices in mathematics instruction. Colorful, imaginative and challenging bulletin boards are ideal for motivating and sustaining interest in mathematics, besides being visual agents for review and reinforcing key principles.

Math Problem of the Week

Reserve a section of the class bulletin board for a "Mathematics Problem of the Week." Both new and experienced teachers can pose interesting mathematical problems that are better suited to bulletin boards. Problems selected should be of a nature that requires more imagination than found in our textbooks.

The slow learner should not be neglected in bulletin board displays. A wise teacher will use a portion of the class bulletin board to display the best work of these pupils. Children, like adults, love to see their work highlighted before an admiring audience. Bulletin boards can foster a greater spirit or neatness and originality in pupils.

When introducing new mathematics units, colorful and thought-provoking bulletin boards, coupled with interesting displays and items of realia, can be the nucleus or springboard for an about-to-be-explored area of the mathematics curriculum.

Making Math Come Alive

It is of vital importance that mathematics, which many children (and adults) find abstract and hard to visualize, be made more meaningful by

Courtesy of Elwood Board of Education, N.Y.

Figure 6-3

Geometric Manipulative Device

carefully planned bulletin boards which show how mathematics is related to everyday living and real situations. For example, appropriate photographs and magazine illustrations can be effective in demonstrating real examples of geometric shapes (Figure 6-3).

PRIMARY BULLETIN BOARD ACTIVITIES

Geometric Funny Faces In cooperation with the art teacher, use a basic geometric shape to create comic and imaginative drawings by children.

"Catch the Ghost" Ask students to draw and cut out simple paper ghosts, goblins and witches, and position them on colored construction paper. Have these spooky apparitions hiding behind tombstones, bushes and a haunted house. Place thereon a short mathematical problem or equation, with unknown factors typed or printed on white paper or oaktag. Ask pupils to capture these evil spirits by supplying the answer. As each student successfully answers the puzzler, he removes the caricature. In other words, in order to remove the ghosts, goblins and witches, pupils must respond correctly to each query.

Picture Collection Teachers, in preparing a bulletin board on such topics as sets, geometry, measurement and fractions, should encourage pupils to bring examples of such concepts and objects. These should be mounted on standard-sized construction paper for display use on the bulletin board.

Geometric Color Posters Ask pupils to make geometric figures, like triangles, rectangles and live segments, from colored straws or pipe cleaners which can be cemented to colored construction paper. Colored yarn could be used to construct closed curves, circles and ovals. A colored felt marker or wax crayon could also be used to outline these geometric shapes. There are pre-packaged flannel board kits in which self-adhering flannel cutouts may be utilized by pupils to form geometric figures (Figure 6-4).

Set Bulletin Board On one side of the bulletin board place a series of illustrations (magazine or drawings) showing sets of objects. On the other side of the bulletin board place numerals or number words. Use colored yarn and thumb tacks to match each picture-set with abstract numerals. This activity may also be performed with equal ease with the aid of a flannel board mathematics kit, such as the Instructo product illustrated in Figure 6-4. Sensitized backing materials on oaktag-mounted magazine illustrations and simple pupil-drawings will successfully augment these commercial flannel cutouts (Figure 6-5).

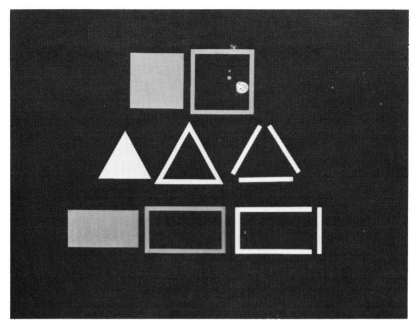

Figure 6-4

Geometric Flannel Figures

Colorful geometric figures can be made by pupils easily at the flannel board.

Figure 6-5

Set Bulletin Board and Flannel Board

Pupil experiences in the concept of mathematical sets can be supplemented by the flannel board.

Numeration Charts Have children use items such as toothpicks, tongue depressors, or cotton swabs, mounted on construction paper to illustrate place value when teaching numeration units.

How Many? Have pupils make drawings in which they mount a specific number of objects and ask members of the class to estimate the number of items.

Math Animals Ask children to use animated drawings that can be cut out to illustrate mathematical sentences or equations. The drawings should be accompanied by letter captions done on construction paper or blank 5 x 8″ cards.

INTERMEDIATE BULLETIN BOARD ACTIVITIES

Travel Bureau Try to construct a social studies poster and bulletin board, showing scenes of interesting places, and outline an itinerary to foreign places. The itinerary should be one that lends itself to computation and exercises in estimation. Travel brochures, readily obtained from local travel bureaus, can be distributed to pupils. Have them form small groups, each responsible for estimating the cost of a trip. Selected pupils in the class could make believe they are planning to take a vacation and are visiting a travel bureau to find out the costs. A colorful geographic bulletin board is an appropriate backdrop for such an activity.

Math Mystery Corner Set up a bulletin board containing some interesting and challenging mathematical problems. In a corner of the bulletin board, answer sheets to problems could be covered until the teacher is ready to divulge the answers to the class or individual pupils. A variation or supplementary activity of this idea is to place, by the bulletin board, a quiz box with mathematical problems printed or typed to sustain interest started.

The History of Math Cooperative pupil-teacher bulletin boards on the history of mathematics, touching on such intriguing and engrossing historically rich mathematical topics as numeration and measurement, would not only make these units more meaningful, but call for a large degree of pupil participation. Such arresting mathematics topics provide the opportunity for challenging library research and creative composition work.

Estimation Collect a series of pictures which will call for pupils to estimate or calculate approximate weight and size of certain living and nonliving things. For example, pictures of such small and large animals as cats and elephants may be mounted on the bulletin board and used to stimulate interest in a lesson in estimating the weights of animals. Inanimate and nonliving objects can also be suitable subjects for estimating, such as the weight of a car compared with that of a child's bicycle.

Newspaper Arithmetic   Both pupil and teacher can collect a series of interesting newspaper ads for mounting on colored construction paper. Advertisements from colorful sections of Sunday newspaper supplements are most attractive. Advertisement charts are placed on the bulletin board to be utilized as a vehicle for making up interesting mathematical problems (Figure 6-6).

Courtesy of Elwood Board of Education, N.Y.

Figure 6-6
Better Math Understanding with Charts

MODELS AND REALIA

Math in Child's Environment

One of the most important teaching functions in mathematics instruction is to make it fascinating and above all, more meaningful. Mathematics is applicable to a child's environment, particularly when we enter such topic areas as geometry and measurement which call for intensive use of models, display and other items of realia; e.g., children obviously can gain much from mathematics when they can construct, see and feel geometric shapes. Likewise, development of dioramas and charts, by the cooperative teamwork of pupil and teacher, is of inestimable value.

Commercial or Homemade Replicas

Of course, we realize there are many commercial manufacturers with professional and polished replicas of items aforementioned. One enter- prising teacher has taught place value by using tongue depressors which are inserted in slits in the bases of 4 x 12″ foam plastic blocks. The slits hold the depressors in place and may be labeled and arranged for place value purposes.

A TYPICAL ACTIVITY WITH MODELS AND REALIA

Geometry Game Time   Distribute to pupils strips of durable oaktag or construction paper along with brass paper fasteners. An enrichment activity, after they have been taught geometric shapes, is to have them make as many manipulatable geometric shapes as possible within a certain time limit. Teams can be set up for game purposes.

CHALKBOARD TECHNIQUES

Long before the advent of the overhead, the chalkboard was the indis- pensable mainstay of mathematics instruction. It still remains one of the key vehicles in explaining mathematical concepts.

Encourage High Degree of Pupil Involvement

One of the major advantages of the chalkboard is that it enables a high degree of pupil participation. Students can readily place their work on a board in full view of the teacher and classmates, and mistakes can be corrected by either pupil or teacher.

Ideal Vehicle for Demonstrating Graphs and Charts

Complicated charts and diagrams may be placed on the chalkboard well in advance of the lesson, and utilized in the actual lesson at the teacher's discretion. Colored chalk makes bar and line graphs, and such geometric shapes as quadrilateral squares and triangles more visually attractive. Templates cut from heavy cardboard or plywood can assist teachers to outline accurate mathematical shapes with greater ease and in less time.

Space on chalkboards can, of course, be reserved for class homework assignments, as a means for reviewing basic mathematical principles, or for student presentations.

To Motivate Interest in Math

Perhaps the basic necessity for the chalkboard, besides explaining mathematics to youngsters, is its importance in motivating interest in this key subject. For example, an addition problem utilizing the provocative Hindu method of addition, or doing addition and subtraction in different number bases, makes for an intriguing introduction to mathematics when presented in a systematic and stimulating style on the chalkboard.

CHALKBOARD ACTIVITIES

Guess the Number   A game well-suited for primary level involves the basic operations of addition and subtraction. The teacher writes a series of mystery numbers which are covered up with paper and tape. Individual pupils try to guess the mystery value on the board as the teacher gives clues, such as numbers in place value and combinations.

Find the Mistake   Place a series of examples on the board, with perhaps one or two containing mistakes. Have the class try to check the work on the examples on scrap paper and see if they can find the errors.

Daily Five   Divide the class into three or four subgroups. Place on the board daily mathematical problems or examples of puzzlers which the whole group does on the chalkboard. Each team scores one point for each correct answer. Let children decide intriguing mathematical names for their respective groups. Charts on each group's progress will breed healthy competition and enliven the mathematics program.

Fraction Fun   Students can develop an interesting panel of drawings on the blackboard representing whole numbers, fractions and mixed numbers. The class can divide into several committees that may assign a series of drawings for a specified collection of numbers. Games may be played in which pupils are asked to name examples of proper and improper fractions.

MEANINGFUL PROCEDURES FOR FILMSTRIPS AND SLIDE MATERIALS

More Versatile Filmstrip and Slide Materials

For a number of years there have been relatively few filmstrips available that could be effectively integrated in a regular elementary mathematics classroom. Fortunately, the manufacturers of these aids have remedied this. Because of the fact that filmstrips are much shorter in length than films, frames of filmstrips can be advanced, reversed, and held at the teacher's discretion, making them generally suitable for mathematics instruction when the appropriate filmstrip is available. In the future, synchronized tape and disc recordings dealing with mathematical concepts and principles will become accessible to schools.

A filmstrip does not require lengthy preparation by the teacher. It is certainly much easier for the teacher to preview a filmstrip more efficiently and take pertinent notes in order to expand the concepts and underline principles that make mathematics discussions more lively.

Mathematics is a subject that requires frequent review. Well-made filmstrips, especially those in color, are an attractive means of accomplishing this task on a class or individual pupil basis. Many commercial filmstrip companies have manuals or guides that contain suggestions for proper use of this visual.

Use, Not Abuse

The important thing for teachers to remember is to utilize filmstrips correctly, usually as an introduction or review on mathematical subjects. To employ filmstrips in themselves as the basis for a lesson is of little educational value. It is particularly important to use mathematics filmstrips for a particular objective, and this objective should be made obvious to the captive audience.

Imaginative Slide Materials

Commercial and noncommercial 2 x 2″ slides are flexible visual devices which can be used graphically to dramatize to the student the practical side of mathematics.

PRIMARY AND INTERMEDIATE ACTIVITIES
USING FILMSTRIPS AND SLIDES

Math Vocabulary   Have student committees or individual pupils preview mathematics filmstrips and list all new mathematical terms. Suggest pupils list these terms on the chalkboard.

Comparison and Evaluation   Encourage class and pupil committees to compare the textbook treatment of a mathematics topic with the filmstrip treatment, with its obvious advantages of magnification and color.

Guess What's Next?   Filmstrips, of course, are arranged in a set sequence, and a sense of continuity is highly important in mathematics instruction. Show a filmstrip, on number bases or expanded notation, in which you show provocative frames; then literally skip a frame or two, and ask pupils to speculate what the intermediate steps might be. After discussion, return to the skipped frames to see how correct or incorrect the class was.

Visualizing Math Slides Combine the best of commercial and non-professional slides to illustrate such mathematical topics as sets and geometric forms. Slides can show practical applications of geometry and mathematics in designs of buildings and bridges. As a follow-up activity, pupils might be encouraged to take pictures with simple cameras of the same objects shown in the slides.

SUMMARY

Math is all around us. We should realize that even our classrooms can become math laboratories. Walls and ceilings, tile floors, desks and doors, all give a pupil numerous opportunities for exercises in measuring and geometry and plain old-fashioned arithmetic.

Audio-visual hardware—such as the tape recorder, overhead projector, filmstrips and slides, bulletin board, displays and realia—can make your classroom a pleasant place for a mathematical experience. In using the materials and hardware about you, never underestimate your own in-genuity and that of your pupils. Children like to pretend and play together, and with the enhancing values of audio-visual materials, math can become an exciting subject, not to just a few, but to everyone.

7

NEW
AUDIO-VISUAL
APPROACHES TO
TEACHING SCIENCE

Aural Teaching Techniques

A great deal of emphasis on aural visual aids in teaching science is concerned with the sounds of nature and the world of science technology. In addition, the tape recorder and disc recording allow us to bring the actual words of famous scientists directly into our classrooms. We may have the students or teacher reflect their own thoughts on tape, perhaps give background information which they have researched in key areas of science, health and safety, or even tape interviews with knowledgeable people in specific science areas from their own and neighboring communities. Certainly, impressions of field trips of a scientific nature can be taped for the purposes of pupil discussion and meaningful review.

The overhead projector opens a whole new world for both pupil and teacher in science. Simple demonstrations can be performed on the stage of the overhead. Commercial and nonprofessional transparencies make it possible for the teacher to help pupils by stages to understand visually difficult science principles. In addition, the teacher, with the overhead, maintains a face-to-face contact with his pupils while what is projected is being explained.

Not only do we have a wide variety of science filmstrips from which to choose, but the majority of teachers will find selections that are not only authentic, but highly informative and appropriate to their grade levels; 2 x 2″ slides, of the commercial and noncommercial variety, provide today's classroom teacher with an additional margin of flexibility and visual motivation for the science curriculum.

Motion pictures are particularly effective for science instruction purposes with such technical assets as time lapse photography, animation and movement, and the undeniable qualities of music and sound. Most educational science films have accompanying manuals that are most helpful in familiarizing the teacher with the content and objectives of the movie. The commercial and educational television science program has, besides all the obvious advantages of the motion picture, the inherent quality of immediacy, which is important in stimulating interest in science. Certainly happenings, such as telecasts of space launchings and live science demonstrations, can add tremendous zest to a science lesson.

The bulletin board, along with the flannel board, can be used in science units in an unlimited number of situations, if introduced and constructively built around an imaginative and thought-provoking theme. Illustrative materials, such as photographs, map illustrations and pupil-drawings, are ideal source material for imaginative bulletin board usage (Figure 7-1).

Photo by Author

Figure 7-1

Typical Science Bulletin Board

Perhaps the most useful audio-visual aids are the near-relatives of the bulletin board: namely, the science model and diorama. Dioramas and models, whether professional or amateur in nature, can be highly effective in providing and recreating significant science experiences and fostering lasting interest in this challenging subject. The diorama kindles an atmosphere of near-reality, a most essential element in meaningful science instruction. Visitors to science and history museums are usually favorably impressed by realistic and timely dioramas. Surely, both children and adults enjoy such vicarious experiences.

AURAL TEACHING TECHNIQUES

Inspired Research Activities

The tape recorder is an inspirational force for a multitude of science research activities. Teachers can prepare a series of science problems in which pupils, in order to resolve the problem, must engage in research. The findings of the research itself can also be placed on tape as a record for all to share in the present and future.

Lasting Impressions of Field Trips

As with social studies field trips, there is a high degree of science interest in visitations to such places as the planetarium, aquarium and science museum. Taped impressions may be either done on the spot during their visitations or as reflections by students on the points of interest of a previous trip. Slides of trips can also be successfully combined with narrative tapes for a more telling effect.

Professional Science Tapes

Teachers should utilize the services of the National Tape Repository, located at the University of Colorado in Boulder, Colorado, for science tapes on such topics as "Alphabet of Science," "Tune in for Health," "A World of Wonders," "Let Science Tell Us," and "The Ocean Depths." (For a more detailed description, check the National Tape Recording Catalog, which may be obtained for $3.00 per copy from the Department of Audiovisual Instruction, NEA, 1201 16th Street, N.W., Washington, D.C. 20036.)

At the primary level the tape recorder is ideal for transcribing oral science book reports which will be appreciated by the pupil's peers. Pupil dramatizations on tape, of space probes and science historical endeavors, are also intriguing ingredients in the audio phase of the science program. In addition, both pupils and teacher, when recorders are available, should record the audio portion of scientific telecasts or educational radio programs with science themes (Figure 7-2).

Courtesy of 3M Company, St. Paul, Minnesota

Figure 7-2

Science Tapes

Listening Corner

Imaginative Commercial Tapes and Recordings

Imperial International Learning (Kankakee, Illinois 60901) has two series of tapes—one for grades 1 to 3, entitled "Let's Find Out," and "Discovery Through Science" for grades 4 to 6—covering such topics as insects, the wheel, plants, sounds, and atoms and molecules.

There are a number of stimulating commercial science records being distributed. One is "The Talking Weather Map" (C. S. Hammond, Maplewood, New Jersey) which skillfully combines a weather chart with a disc recording. Another commendable science series is "Signposts for Young Scientists," a Folkways/Scholastic Record album (50 West 44th St., New York, N.Y. 10036). This is a five-record set dealing with such subjects as life's beginnings, inventions, planets, conservation and wild life.

Sounds of science which are all about us, from the happy chirp of robin redbreast to the call of the crow, can be put down on a tape recording. The sounds of machines and musical instruments on records can make a good spinoff for a fascinating science lesson.

PRIMARY AURAL ACTIVITIES

Mystery Sounds   The teacher or individual pupils can record a series of related or unrelated sounds for the class to try to identify. This activity can be used as a lead-in to meaningful science discussions.

Way-Out Science Stories   After listening to records about outer space and extra-terrestrial life beyond the stars, have pupils plan to write scripts or stories to be dramatized on the tape recorder. Perhaps a future H. G. Wells may be awaiting the attention of an anxious world. Have a class discussion on the difference between scientific fact and science fiction (Figure 7-3).

Weather Bureau   Have pupils bring in clippings from newspapers giving the weather forecast for a specific day. Use recordings taped from radio and television programs for the same day. Encourage the class to analyze the degree of accuracy of these forecasts and the probable reasons for any discrepancy.

INTERMEDIATE AURAL ACTIVITIES

Voice Analysis   Plan to use recordings of various adult and children's voices, as an introduction to the mechanics of how man communicates, as well as for a discussion of the physical mechanics of how one speaks.

Figure 7-3

Illustration by Mary Farrell

"Way Out" Science Stories—The Martians Are Coming!

The Interview of the Week Have a committee of pupils prepare a series of questions for the purpose of interviewing the dental hygiene teacher, the school nurse, or perhaps the family physician—if they are not too busy. Appoint a committee of pupils to conduct the interviews.

OPAQUE AND OVERHEAD PROJECTOR

The opaque has a wide range of uses as a visual aid for science. It may be gainfully used as a visual device for illustrating points in a teacher's science lesson or in highlighting a pupil's science report. The opaque can effectively spotlight science diagrams prepared by pupils. Simple chemical changes and reactions may be viewed by the class when chemicals are placed in a flat dish such as a petri dish.

Testing Recall

Examinations on the identification of animals, birds and leaves may be efficiently administered with the opaque projector. Before testing the pupils, show and identify each picture or write its name on the board for note-taking purposes. Encourage pupils taking notes to make short, pertinent comments which help them recall each item clearly for a test.

Do not hesitate to use the opaque projector itself as a piece of scientific apparatus for instruction in vision or optics. Various parts can be analyzed, such as its lens system, reflectors and projection lamp, to be used as the nucleus for a lesson on light.

Small scientific and specific 3-dimensional items, such as rocks or shells, can be projected readily with the opaque projector. This allows the whole class to view these objects as they are discussed.

Overhead—a Science Laboratory

The ever-versatile overhead projector readily converts to a science "lab." Numerous experiments can be performed on the stage of the overhead projector; for example, lay a glass plate and magnet thereon and sprinkle iron filings on the glass plate; the projected result shows clearly that the filings definitely form a magnetic field (Figure 7-4).

Courtesy of Charles Beseler Company, East Orange, N.J.

Figure 7-4

Showing a Magnetic Field on the Overhead

Unique Polaroid Experimentation

Polarization of light experiments utilizing glass material obtained from the Polaroid Company (730 Main St., Cambridge, Massachusetts 02142), make fascinating science experiments. One simple means of demonstrating polarized light is to arrange Scotch Tape in a criss-cross pattern on a piece of glass or acetate. By revolving the polarizing material, vivid rainbow color effects are achieved. Otherwise, a wad of crumbled cellophane on an overhead projector stage may be used for demonstrations of polarization.

One intriguing lab technique for demonstrating sound patterns is accomplished by placing a clear pyrex dish of water on the stage of the overhead. Strike a tuning fork, and touch it to the water in the dish. Watch the rippling water as it rebounds on the sides of the shallow dish. The rebounding water represents sound wave patterns. By placing different articles in the dish, other interesting patterns may be viewed on the screen (from an idea practiced by numerous science teachers in the Long Island and Connecticut areas).

Weather maps, made on simple outline map transparencies with overlays indicating pertinent weather symbols, temperatures and air mass movements, are well-suited for science lessons. Later, have children who are familiar with the subject bring newspaper weather maps, or those from such sources as the U.S. Weather Bureau, for class discussion.

Demonstrate concepts like surface tension on the overhead stage by dropping a small amount of oil or detergent into the water. Pupils will be fascinated by the results of this action when magnified on the classroom screen.

To Explain the Inclined Plane

Understanding of inclined planes can be clarified by laying screws and bolts on the overhead projector to magnify them approximately seven times their size. Questions such as, "What is the number of threads per inch?" and "What are the names of some of the other examples of inclined plane we may find in our environment?" may be asked of students.

You can also demonstrate the difference between Centigrade and Fahrenheit thermometers by projecting these two thermometers via the stage of the overhead projector. Indicate the same temperature on both thermometers when placed side by side on the overhead.

Indeed the overhead is an indispensable teaching aid in fulfilling today's demands for imaginative and attention-gathering science teaching.

OPAQUE AND OVERHEAD ACTIVITIES

Science Crossword Puzzle   Have older pupils submit short crossword puzzles which can be made into transparencies. A supplementary aid to this activity is to ditto copies of puzzles so that everyone is involved in solving the puzzle.

The Effects of Erosion   Have children collect a series of pictures from magazines or make drawings showing the effects of wind and rain in creating conditions of erosion. A series of illustrations showing the effects of storms as tornadoes or cyclones, can also be an interesting topic for the opaque projector. The pictures should be mounted on oaktag, labeled with the Magic Marker and displayed on the bulletin board.

Scavenger Hunt   Have individual pupils collect any interesting and suitable scientific items for overhead projection; observe some form of recognition for the best science item contributed.

FILMSTRIPS AND SLIDES

Instant Action and Reaction

The science filmstrip has been increasing in popularity among classroom teachers. A good science slidefilm will not only control a pupil's interest, but—highly important—it will certainly foster immediate feelings of action and reaction from the students as individuals, as well as from the group as a whole.

It is particularly important in science, where a concept is being illustrated or principle proven, or where an experiment is being shown, to be able to control the time and the amount of attention given to a sequence of factual information or directed to a specific fact in science.

The printed narrative that accompanies most filmstrips often contains a series of questions which not only motivates discussions, but is an ideal tool for review. Science filmstrips, as in all subject areas, should be carefully integrated into the lesson, rather than becoming the lesson itself.

Filmstrips set the stage for pupil activities, particularly in the area of scientific research. For example, a filmstrip based on a space launching or a trip to the moon can inspire student reports and encourage the creation of exciting dioramas depicting a rocket launching or perhaps a lunar landscape.

Ideal Source for Information and Ideas

Filmstrip manuals and the filmstrips themselves contain ideas for science discussion, as well as suggesting demonstrations that pupils can perform readily. Of course, a preview of a science filmstrip helps not only to supply the new, but the experienced teacher with an excellent informational background for evolving a "solid" science lesson plan.

Science filmstrips can be a definite asset prior to a scientific field trip as well as a sound method of review to follow up a worthwhile field trip. Questions may be posed before the trip which are specifically answered or left unanswered during the trip. Perhaps the filmstrip could not supply the answer, either, after the visitation, but its reviewing of points can give impetus to further research which may be more productive.

Filmstrips Enhance Science Demonstrations

Many skillful teachers have coupled the science filmstrip with pupil or teacher science demonstrations to effectively teach the scientific method. For example, have an older pupil project several frames of filmstrips on magnetism or condensation as an introduction to the topic. Next, have the student indicate the principle he wishes to demonstrate, and have him perform the actual experiment before the class. Later, allow the student experimentor to make his own conclusions as to the results of the experiment.

Another unique technique employed by enterprising New Jersey teachers is to utilize the projector to produce spirit or duplicator masters. This is accomplished by projecting an image directly on the spirit master, then carefully tracing the image on the master. The final step is the actual running of the ditto master in the conventional way.

The filmstrip projector may be combined with a phonograph turntable to demonstrate the earth's rotation. This is achieved by making a small flag, out of a piece of paper and pin, which is then attached to a globe that is seated on a phonograph turntable. The filmstrip projector is then placed in such a position that its light brightens one side of the globe. Start the projector and phonograph running, and alert the class to how the flag moves in and out of the shadow of the rotating earth. The class may be queried as to why half the globe always remains dark, or why the flag is sometimes illuminated and yet sometimes dark.

There is never a shortage of science filmstrip material. All manufacturers of filmstrips have an ample library available in this area as an examination of any of their catalogs will attest. Manufacturers like Eye Gate House, Jam Handy, Encyclopaedia Britannica, McGraw-Hill and the Society of Visual Education are only too willing to send you or your school a catalog of their product. *The Educator's Guide to Free Slide Films* (Educator Progress Service) and *Educational Media Index* (McGraw-Hill) contain information on the desirable filmstrip. *Educa-*

tional Screen AV Guide has a monthly filmstrip review feature by Dr. Irene Cypher. *Grade Teacher* has had a regular service feature by Dr. Edward E. Miller and Mrs. Barbara D. Miller, which reviews the newest filmstrip releases in addition to film and record releases.

Let's not neglect the role of the commercial and non-professional 35mm transparencies for animal and plant analysis, and for visual source examples of erosion. Nonprofessional 2 x 2″ slides, taken by teachers or parents in their homes, are excellent for showing the uses of electricity or perhaps how food is prepared and preserved.

FILMSTRIP AND SLIDE ACTIVITIES

Safety and Experiment Slides   A good discussion of playground, bus or school safety by pupils could lead to a set of key ideas and rules on safety. Many of today's 35mm cameras are simple to operate because most of the trouble spots in photography are lessened by the automatic range finder and electric eye, thus making it easy for the teacher and pupil to take their own slides.

How to Experiment   Another idea closely related to safety slides is to take a series of slides of either a science experiment or of living and non-living objects and ask pupils at random to give a capsule three-minute recapitulation of the experiment or demonstration shown.

Why?   Show a single frame of a filmstrip without the caption. Let the pupils explain what they think is happening in the final frame as well as calling upon students to cite other examples of situations in which the scientific principle being seen applies.

See and Draw   Improved scientific drawing, in addition to supplying visual practice in recalling the labels of a scientific chart, can be enhanced by flashing a frame of the filmstrip on the screen for a full minute or more; after which let the pupils draw the sketches. Then turn on the projector and see how accurate their drawings are.

MOTION PICTURES AND TELEVISION

Teachers are indeed fortunate to have the chance to select from numerous educational science films or some of the outstanding sponsored films, such as the widely acclaimed Bell Telephone System series, hosted by Frank Baxter, "Our Mr. Sun" and "Hemo, the Magnificent."

Better Learning via the Magic of Photography

Movies, with their skillful use of time lapse photography, microphotography, animation and the added obvious dimension of motion and sound, make science a truly exciting experience. For instance, time lapse photography enables the viewers to see in a matter of a few minutes what in actuality took several days or hours to take place; i.e., a flower opening or the chrysalis of a butterfly. These attributes can be most helpful in stimulating class discussion and clarifying difficult-to-teach scientific concepts (Figures 7-5 and 7-6).

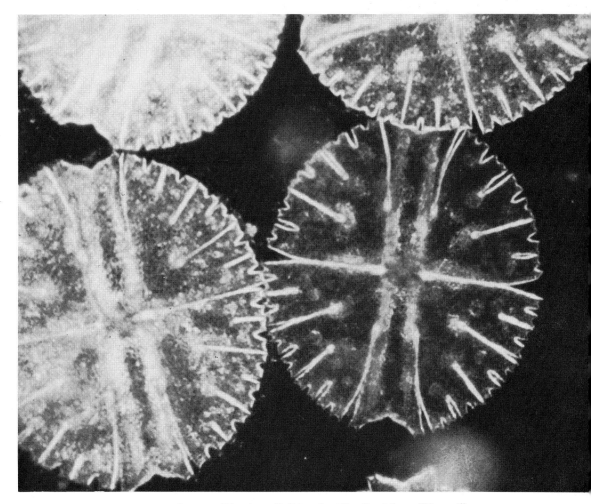

Courtesy of Encyclopaedia Britannica, Educational Corp., Chicago, Ill.

Figure 7-5
The Use of Microphotography in Science Films
A scene from the film, "Microscopic Life: The World of the Invisible"

Courtesy of Coronet Instructional Films, Chicago, Ill.

Figure 7-6

The Use of Microphotography in Science Films

Primary Science Film: "Insects and Their Homes"

Science movies must be previewed for various reasons. First, the teacher must decide whether the subject matter and vocabulary is suitable to the group viewing the movies. A preview enables the teacher to plan lessons with a purpose and to provide the appropriate atmosphere and readiness for the group.

Teaching with Film

Re-showing worthwhile science films is comparable to re-reading a textbook for the purpose of review and retention. Actually, films often contain many visuals to command the viewer's attention. Running a motion picture without sound, or stopping a film at a pre-determined point, is not to be frowned upon; on the contrary, this practice should be encouraged as it can be an asset in making pertinent points or posing thought-provoking questions.

MOTION PICTURE AND TELEVISION ACTIVITIES

Nature Log   After watching a motion picture or television program dealing with plant and animal life, ask pupils to prepare a nature log. This would be a record of personal observations related to the subject viewed in the film.

Science Film Review   Ask the class to prepare a short description on what they have seen in the film. If the film has an overabundance of technical details, select a segment for written description or comments. Prepare an illustration or drawing to accompany the written assignment.

Watch and Do   If the film shows a simple experiment of an activity that can be dramatized, have pupils re-enact what they have seen while the details are still fresh in their minds.

Science Panel Forum   If the subject of a science film covers a scientific field such as conservation, oceanography, space exploration and modern technology, an interesting panel discussion could result (Figure 7-7).

Illustration by Mary Farrell

Figure 7-7
Science Panel Forum

Now Playing Have pupils sketch a series of drawings on waxed or crayonized paper to illustrate key science principles or concepts. Then insert the waxed paper roll in a cardboard box. A portion of the carton will have to be cut away to provide an opening for the screen, which is the moving roll of waxed paper containing the drawings. A wooden dowel will help the roll of waxed paper turn more readily.

BULLETIN, FLANNEL AND CHALKBOARD

The Vehicle for Research and Problem Solving

An eye-catching, neatly arranged science bulletin board should be an integral part of every classroom and be carefully woven into the fabric of each new science unit. There are different types of science bulletin boards. One is built around developing science displays which, by featuring magazine and newspaper articles of science happenings, sustain pupil interest and promote study in research, science projects and scholarship.

Another successful type of bulletin board, which should yield good educational results, is a problem-oriented bulletin board. This kind of visual can pose provocative questions that call for reflective thinking, reading, listening and researching on the student's part. An extension of the problem-oriented display is to *be* functional and show steps in the solution of specific science principles or problems.

There is no lack of themes for the science bulletin board. They can be centered around such diverse subjects as the seasons, safety, health, astronomy, or animal and plant life. The science bulletin board can have more impact when used in concert with supplemental models, specimens and pupil-made dioramas.

Pupil participation in setting up a series of productive bulletin boards in this subject area is a must. Students should be asked to contribute interesting magazine and newspaper illustrations, and photographs that they or their parents have taken. Pupils' art work, diagrams or sketches having relevancy to scientific topics to be studied should be encouraged.

Graphic Bulletin Boards

Many experienced teachers have found that taking pictures and photographs for the bulletin board is an instantaneous visual means of recall, the ingredient for a successful display. These photographs, with accompanying notes by the teacher, can be filed for future reference.

The flannel board and magnetic chalkboard are also productive instructional relatives of the bulletin board and are particularly helpful in the primary grade level in explaining a scientific process or set of principles, or demonstrating theories. For example, properly mounted and flannel-backed cutouts can be used to teach the growth of plants from seed to flower. Likewise, well-planned science diagrams on a chalkboard can clarify functions and relationships in science that might take a teacher many hours to explain by words alone.

Teachers should employ the flannel or felt board as an instructional device to display science flow charts. It is recommended that this pre-pared material be stored from year to year in separate envelopes and cataloged by the teacher. The charts can be made from oaktag and printed with a Magic Marker.

Star constellations may be shown on the flannel board. With younger children it may be utilized in relating the fascinating mythology asso-ciated with these constellations. At the intermediate level, flannel boards can be utilized to interpret and explain molecular and atomic structure. More sophisticated and ambitious flannel board diagrams cannot help but enhance a science lesson.

BULLETIN BOARD, FLANNEL BOARD AND CHALKBOARD ACTIVITIES

Well-Balanced Meal   Teacher and pupils can use commercially-made or their own flannel-backed cutouts of foods from drawings or magazine illustrations to demonstrate the contents of a well-balanced meal.

"I See Stars"   Here is an activity for astronomy-minded teachers and pupils. Plan to use the opaque or overhead projector to make an out-line of interesting constellations directly on a bulletin board covered with plain white construction or drawing paper. Indicate more clearly each star's position by employing straight pins pushed through gummed stars. Colored yarn or cord can also be used to dramatize the visual pattern of these star constellations.

Dino, the Silhouetted Dinosaur   Children of all ages are intrigued with dinosaurs; make this fascination work for you in science. Make a bulletin board with various dinosaur silhouettes. The silhouettes may be traced with the aid of the opaque or overhead projector. Black construc-tion paper is perhaps the best material to use for effective silhouettes, although other colors might conceivably be used. Ferns and other tropical vegetation may be made from green construction paper or crepe paper as an enhancing backdrop for the silhouettes (Figure 7-8).

Today's Weather Forecast   With a series of weather pictures and illus-trations, have the class prepare various weather conditions. Use colored

Illustration by Mary Farrell

Figure 7-8
Dino, the Silhouetted Dinosaur

yarn and tie the yarn, from the picture that shows the correct weather condition, to the tag that also indicates the weather for the day.

Fuels Chart   Encourage pupils to prepare a chart of common fuels. Oil, coal, gas and other fuels are believed to be the remains of animals and greens. It will be interesting to trace the energy of particular refined fuels such as gasoline right back to the sun.

DIORAMAS, MODELS, REALIA AND PROJECTS

Effective visual aids, in the form of student-made dioramas, models, collections, or realia and projects, have become increasingly popular with both the pupil and teacher in science. The wonders of the scientific world are all about us, so why not make science more significant and realistic to your pupils by helping them recreate this environment?

Sources for Diorama Ideas

There are a hundred different methods and approaches to diorama and model construction. Some of the more reliable pamphlet sources for detailed teacher information on preparing science and social studies dioramas are Dorothy H. Curries' *Making Dioramas and Displays* (F. A. Owen Publishing Company, Dansville, N.Y.) and *Bridges for Ideas— Models for Teaching* (University of Texas, Austin, Texas); some simple tips on the construction of dioramas are contained in the chapter on social studies.

Solid models of animals or insects, exact models such as an electric motor or enlarged model of a human cell, cut-away sections of the human body, or a working model telegraph—all make science instruction not only visually informative, but afford the pupil a dynamic and rewarding introduction to any science theme. Pupils also enjoy making their own working models, such as simple electric circuits, bells or homemade replicas of simple machines, like the early cotton gin or press. Teachers should assist their students by having them compile illustrated reference materials from textbooks, magazines or catalog charts to have as guidelines for the construction of the model. With older children you might stress the importance of perspective and scale in achieving accuracy.

The opaque projector is particularly useful for the purpose of magnifying a drawing or photograph which is being used as a guideline for the actual construction of a model. Filmstrips and slides add to the fund of necessary knowledge.

In making scientific models and dioramas, details of the original should be uncomplicated, and if nonessential, left out. However, caution must be exercised to avoid distortion. Commercial and pupil-constructed models should meet specific teaching objectives and be tailored to the appropriate age group with which you are working.

A trip to a planetarium, aquarium, zoo or science museum would help pupils gain a tremendous amount of background information otherwise not available through books and other media. In constructive science dioramas and models, each project should be accompanied by oral or written explanations. Encourage pupils to set aside an appropriate time in developing their explanations. A wise teacher can test the clarity of each pupil's explanation by the class discussion that follows.

A source for motivational science activities is the booklet "Science Games and Activities," by Wagner, Duea, Finsand, Mork, and published by Teachers Publishing Corporation, Darien, Conn. 06820.

DIORAMAS AND RELATED ACTIVITIES

Don't Be a Slouch!   Make your class conscious of poor habits of sitting and standing. Encourage pupils to mold clay human figures to demonstrate good posture habits. Some teachers have found that ordinary pipe cleaners make excellent figures to demonstrate these poses. Accompany these figures with short talks and stick-figure sketches of bad posture.

Safety Diorama Have pupils with either colored Mystic Tape, Magic Marker or paint, lay out patterns for streets on cardboard, plywood or oaktag. Place toy model cars, stick figures and cardboard cutouts on the layout in positions demonstrating good and poor safety habits. Girls with toy doll houses and furniture could also illustrate, with a diorama, needed safety rules in the home.

They Came from Outer Space Divide the class into two committees. Have one committee construct, from clay, moon people or Martian monsters. These creatures can be placed in a shoebox with a simply drawn moon or Martian landscape. Have the space committee tell wide-eyed stories of these strange beings. The job of the other committees is to disprove, by a variety of scientific evidence, that these beings probably exist only in the fertile imagination of science fiction "writers."

Young Folks Science Corner Start a permanent display of science items that kindergarteners can handle safely, such as pulleys, magnets, batteries, scales and balances, hourglasses, flashlights, old clocks and bells. Do not force the children to explain or understand how they function. The idea is to *motivate* your pupil with such science materials.

Junior Scientists A good activity to create interest in laboratory science is to have children study a simple earthworm. Have youngsters compare size of worms and variations in color. With a magnifying glass, study the segments in the worm's body. The teacher can then discuss how worms aerate the soil and their role in nature's scheme. Have the children make drawings of the earthworm (Figure 7-9).

Egg Shell Garden Try an egg shell garden. Paint egg shells bright colors; then fill shells with soil. Next, plant small seeds, place the eggs in an old egg carton, water daily, and watch the garden grow.

Save a Leaf To preserve leaves, place a leaf between two pieces of waxed paper and press down on the sandwich with a warm iron. If done correctly, the leaf should be coated with a fine layer of wax. Caution: let the children collect and classify leaves, but only a teacher should use the hot iron in preparing the leaves for preservation.

Individualized Terrarium Projects To make a class terrarium or aquarium, consult good science teachers' manuals which describe how terrariums are constructed. They also give sound advice on the care of an aquarium and inspire groups of children to make smaller replicas of it.

Fossil Prints Make fossil prints from simple mold forms and plaster of Paris. Use vaseline so that castings can be removed from the mold easily.

Mount Vesuvius Spectacular One student attention-getter is a home-made replica of Mount Vesuvius. It can be readily constructed from

Courtesy of "Our Schools," Board of Education, Northport, N.Y.

Figure 7-9
Junior Scientists

117

plaster of Paris or a composition of paper pulp with paste or size. Either mixture can be molded around chicken wire within which a mailing tube is centered. When the mold dries, it should be painted appropriate volcano colors. The volcano can be depicted in a quiescent or live state. The interior of the abyss should be fitted with crinkled foil. To achieve an eye-catching eruption, load the lined abyss with varying layers of ammonium dichromate and iron filings. Some teachers find that using a mixture of baking soda and vinegar will simulate a simple satisfactory eruption. As a safety precaution, it is imperative that this mixture be ignited by the teacher. By utilizing this working Mount Vesuvius model, many desirable enrichment activities can be effectively inspired.

SUMMARY

Today's trend in elementary science is toward the problem solving and pupil discussion techniques and away from the traditional and often interest-killing lecture and demonstration. A wise teacher will attempt to make his children do the thinking so that lessons and questions come from the class. The world of audio-visual materials helps the classroom teacher to initiate new and different approaches to science instruction, one that fosters pupil curiosity and, at the same time, accumulates a greater degree of scientific knowledge. Audio-visual science aids and techniques do not displace the able classroom teacher, but they do allow pupils to understand how separate scientific theories and concepts can be brought together to form a complete and real picture of science in the world about them.

8

THE IMAGINATIVE
USE OF
AUDIO-VISUAL
AIDS IN THE
SOCIAL STUDIES PROGRAM

Pupil interest will never slacken if the elementary school social studies program can be infused with the imaginative employment of such productive aural tools as the tape recorder and the disc recorder.

Highlights of field trips can be relived, historic events can be dramatized and recreated, and tape "exchanges" on social studies topics with children from other lands offer endless possibilities for effective social science learning techniques. Radio and commercial records can be the springboard for a series of instructional experiences. Both of these audio-visual devices may be used as a means to gain insight into the music, customs and history of our country and other lands.

No one can deny the importance of maps and globes in the geographic phase of a social studies program, as obviously an understanding of a nation's history and progress depends upon an intuitive look at its resources, climate and geographic features.

Graphics, including magazine pictures and photographs, can be dramatically utilized to enhance social studies lessons when projected with the opaque projector with its power of magnification. Transparencies of political cartoons, drawing a time line, and tracing of map routes are a random sampling of a multiplicity of ideas with which the overhead may be used.

The filmstrip is well-suited for instruction, as well as for motivating group or individual social studies research. Professionally-made 2 x 2″ slides, like its filmstrip counterpart, are an unlimited source for productive social studies lessons. Non-professional slides taken by the teacher and pupils can be utilized independently or combined with professional slides as the basis for fascinating social studies instruction.

Motion pictures, live television, and kinescopes can bring the historic events of the past and present directly into the classroom. These dramatic and visually appealing media give a dynamic impetus to the entire program.

As in most subject areas, the bulletin board, flannel board and diorama are the nucleus for numerous pupil-teacher activities and lessons. Dioramas have captured the imagination of young and old at historical museums and restorations for years. Likewise, well-made dioramas can be the focal point of attention in the social studies classroom.

TAPE RECORDER, RECORDS AND RADIO

Tape Recorder a Confidence Builder

Perhaps the most obvious idea, in using the tape recorder with primary school children, is to have each child relate on tape his experiences in traveling. Since some pupils may hesitate to speak into a microphone before the class, the teacher should take these bashful ones aside and spend a few minutes putting them at ease by chatting with them and offering words of encouragement.

Most primary grade field trips are to local points of interest. A recorder could be used to tape the voices of the guide or any key persons who may be speaking to the group while on the tour. What a wonderful review of the field trip, when you can play back the words of the officials of the fire department, the police department and the library!

In the fourth, fifth and sixth grades, children can be grouped into committees and assigned various geographical or historical topics. For each, have one child appointed as chairman. After each committee has thoroughly researched its topic and organized its report, one or all of the group may record their findings. The beauty of the tape recorder is that if someone makes a mistake delivering his report, it can be erased and the report re-recorded. Each committee and the teacher can critically evaluate each report by previewing it, before playing the finished product in front of the entire class.

More mature interviews can be conducted with social studies resource people by older children. A responsible student, with some teacher supervision, could prepare a list of questions for the authority to be interviewed about his field. The student would be responsible for making all arrangements for the time and place for the interviews and should be courteous enough to send a tentative list of questions to the resource person ahead of time. Of course, the finished recording should be replayed for the authority before it is heard in the class.

Commercial Prerecorded Tape Sources

The value of the tape recorder is enhanced by the availability of pre-recorded tapes. Besides the regular commercial sources of tapes, there is the NEA sponsored National Tape Repository at the University of Colorado, a catalog listing a variety of subjects available presently at $3.00 per copy. The tapes are duplicated at a nominal fee, the expense depending on the time length of the tape and recorded on $\frac{1}{4}''$ tapes at $3\frac{3}{4}$ I.P.S. *The Educational Media Index,* published by the McGraw-Hill Company, is still another source of information. It would be very helpful to check with nearby colleges, universities and instructional materials centers for their listings.

World Tapes for Education

One of the most exciting programs in teaching social studies, involves the exchanging of tapes. The most renowned organization involved in this project is the World Tapes for Education. This company encourages the swapping of tapes between class groups all around the world. WTE also publishes an informative, bi-monthly newspaper, called "Tape Topics," which contains numerous articles from tape pals from such countries as Australia, England, Israel, Norway and South Africa. In order to participate in WTE, the teacher must have access to a tape recorder. Surprisingly enough, tape recorder speeds and tracks are standardized all over the world. A three-inch reel of $1\frac{1}{2}$ or 1 mil thickness is used. WTE has a teacher service committee to assist schools that need help in getting the program initiated. For complete information on membership fees, it is recommended that you contact the World Tapes for Education organization, P.O. Box 18703, Dallas, Texas (Figure 8-1).

Educational Screen *Tape Exchange Program*

The publication *Educational Screen and Audiovisual Guide* has also promoted a similar tape exchange program under the guidance of Ruth Y. Terry of Muskegon, Michigan. From time to time the magazine prints names of people abroad who express interest in exchanging tapes with someone in the United States. *Educational Screen* recommends that their readers contact directly the persons listed in their publication. The

Courtesy of World Tapes for Education, Dallas, Texas

Figure 8-1

Students of Mrs. W. Bean, 9 Vernon St., Concord, New Hampshire, prepared a 15-minute tape/slide show on "The Making of Maple Sugar which was well received by their tape contacts in other countries.

A copy of this T/S Show is available from WTE, as they donated it to the organization.
Left to right: Jane Dyment, Ann Niswander, and Julie Jordan.

opening letter should contain pertinent information, such as the name of the school and its location and a description of its equipment.

If you enroll in any type of tape exchange program, the teacher must guide the class in the choice of subjects to be recorded for their tape pal abroad. Children are usually interested in what other children like. The tape program should be well-organized and orally rehearsed numerous times, with all the participants involved. Above all, tapes should have that personal "Getting to Know You" touch, if both parties to the exchange are going to derive any benefit or interest.

Wide Assortment of Social Studies Records

The variety of records for social studies purposes includes dramatizations and re-enactments of significant historical happenings, and other recordings that contain the actual voices of famous personalities. Teachers are fortunate to be able to obtain with ease authentic records based on the music, folklore and culture of America, as well as those of our world neighbors.

It would be an almost impossible task to enumerate the tremendous selection of records becoming available to elementary classrooms. Most record manufacturers, including Decca, Columbia, R.C.A., Capitol, M.G.M. and Folkways, will be glad to send free catalogs of their educational records. More and more record companies are associated with or are an integral part of educational publishing concerns; therefore, many records are carefully correlated to printed texts.

A Glimpse into the Past

Important historical events impressively recreated on records derived from the famed John F. Kennedy television series "Profiles in Courage," are presently being distributed by R.C.A. Record Division, 155 E. 24th St., New York, N.Y. 10010. Enrichment Teaching Materials, 246 Fifth Avenue, New York, N.Y. 10001, also has had an imaginative series of records dramatizing such episodes in American history as "Columbus' Discovery of America," the "Gold Rush" and the "Pony Express."

An exciting idea for social studies lessons is the use of recordings of the actual voices of prominent people and transcriptions of historical events recorded at the time they happened. Columbia Records continues to distribute Edward R. Murrow's ever-popular series "I Can Hear It Now," which traces newsworthy events from 1933 to 1945. Two additional volumes have been released covering the periods 1917 to 1932, and 1945 to 1950. Family Weekly Books, 641 Lexington Ave., New York, N.Y., has a two-volume L.P. album titled "History Speaks," containing the real voices of such personalities as Florence Nightingale, Amelia Earhart, Theodore Roosevelt, Charles Lindbergh, President McKinley and Admiral Peary.

Learning Through Folk Music

We are indeed fortunate to have a great array of folk song recording artists, such talented persons as Burl Ives, Woody Guthrie and Pete Seeger. An outstanding record of this type is "Lonesome Valley," with selections by Tom Glazer, Bess Lomax and Woody Guthrie. Children are often amazed that there is such a wide difference between the original folk song rendition and today's hackneyed Tin Pan Alley version of the same composition.

Learning Social Studies Through Recorded Poetry

Many interesting social studies lessons can be based on America's historical past and present. We have Columbia Records' (Education Dept., Pitman, New Jersey) "America the Beautiful, the Heart of America in Poetry," spoken by Vincent Price; "Poems of My Country," including these selections read by José Ferrer, "Columbus," "The Concord Hymn," "Paul Revere's Ride" and "O Captain! My Captain!", produced by Bowmar Records, North Hollywood, California.

Folkways of Englewood Cliffs, New Jersey, has produced "Of Poetry and Power," read by Irene Daly and Martin Donegan. This recording includes a speech about poetry and its effect on our society by John F. Kennedy. They also have a recording entitled, "Negro Poetry for Young People," an anthology narrated by Arna Bontemps, including poems by Langston Hughes, Paul L. Dunbar, and Countee Cullen. Another series on social studies is their "American History in Ballad and Song, Vol. 1," prepared by Albert Barouh and Theodore O. Cron, with a 24-page teaching guide, chronologically covering the period from Colonial America to America as an expanding power.

A particularly imaginative teaching record that makes map reading an enjoyable experience for third and fourth graders is "Talking Map" by the C. S. Hammond company of Maplewood, New Jersey. It combines a colorful wall map of the world with an informative recorded explanation of its various climatic zones.

There are many fine programs beamed over non-commercial radio networks, such as New York's Empire State FM School of the Air. Many major cities in the United States have an educational radio outlet, and most of them provide teachers' manuals for their subscribers.

As was necessary in the language arts area, there are some important points to remember when you utilize the radio in social studies. A good radio lesson requires a certain degree of subject readiness or background prior to the program. A teacher, previous to the scheduled broadcast, could list on the chalkboard a series of questions dealing with the social studies topic which might be answered during the course of the program. List challenging queries that remind the children that they are listening to a program with a specific purpose. At the conclusion, check with the class to see how many questions were answered. Augment the radio feature with a good filmstrip, library research or recordings. Special follow-up exercises for homework could be used to extend the experience.

AURAL ACTIVITIES

PRIMARY ACTIVITIES

Folklore Geography   There are on the market fine recordings on such colorful legendary American folk heroes as Paul Bunyan, John Henry, Pecos Bill and Davy Crockett. These recordings can be used as the jumping off place for studying the geographic regions from which these stories originated (Figure 8-2).

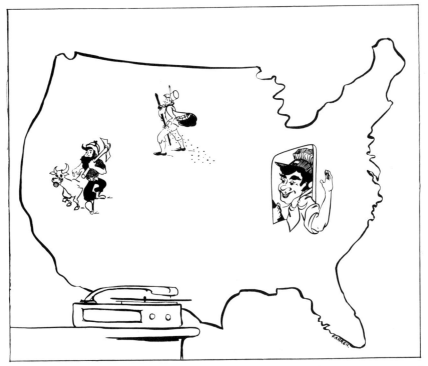

Illustration by Mary Farrell

Figure 8-2
Folklore-Geography

American Indian Unit   The primary curriculum often includes a study of the American Indian. A unit could be evolved on Indian folklore and customs, utilizing a record like Folkway's "Music of the Sioux and the Navajo," (33⅓ rpm) or R.C.A.'s "Music of American Indians," the latter obtained on either 78 or 45 rpm records.

"Guess Who" in History   Another method utilizing the tape recorder, is a game in which a pupil records a short description of a famous person without identifying him. This is played back and everyone tries to guess the identity of the historical celebrity.

Let's Have a Play   Recordings of the music of pioneer America could serve as a spark for preparing simple pantomime and puppetry recreating the heroic days and deeds of Daniel Boone and Davy Crockett. Tape recordings of the children's reactions to the music could be captured on the tape recorder. Recordings of pupil-written plays and poems may also be used.

INTERMEDIATE ACTIVITIES

Press Conference   Turn the usual current events into a radio news conference. Have one pupil act as spokesman, while the others, as questioning newsmen, "cover" news events. Other dramatizations could be patterned after programs similar to the famed radio and television series "Meet the Press." The entire proceedings should be taped for combined learning experiences in social studies and language.

Newsbeat   Have a group of pupils, provided with a lightweight portable tape recorder, act as on-the-spot newscasters who describe real events seen on television. Pupils visiting historic shrines or attending special events, may tape items they consider of local significance, or newsworthy and of interest to the class.

Personalized Tape Exchange   Some teachers may prefer to organize a tape exchange on their own. Contacts might be made by compiling a list of names and activity addresses culled from magazine and newspaper articles, or perhaps through some organization affiliated with the United Nations.

MAPS AND GLOBES

A wide range of maps and globes are available to teachers, maps and globe materials priced to fit almost any budget and teaching situation. Generally, low-priced maps and globes, if employed intelligently, can do a superior job in contrast to elaborate map materials that are utilized in a totally unimaginative manner. Perhaps the best and least expensive map and globe aids are teacher-pupil constructed; more often than not, they can stimulate a greater interest in learning than those which are bought. Of course, the student-teacher map and globe project cannot always achieve the high degree of accuracy and sophistication that is possible with professional materials.

Commercially produced maps and globes cover a highly diversified field of geographic subject matter. They depict political, historical, climatic, topographic and population data in a graphically pleasing fashion. Modern maps and globes are truly versatile. Many of these materials have surfaces which can be marked with chalk and grease pencils or tempera paint, and later wiped or washed clear with a soft or wet cloth (Figure 8-3). Practically all map and globe manufacturers catalog their materials according to grade level. In addition, most companies readily provide teachers' manuals with numerous suggestions and activities for using their products.

Figure 8-3
Children Learn from a Graphic Project Globe
Child is marking the surface of this modern globe with chalk.

Courtesy A. J. Nystrom & Co., Chicago, Ill.

Although maps and globes are considered companion teaching tools, the globe still remains as the most preferred type of map since it represents directions, distances, shapes and areas in better perspective than flat maps.

Symbols the Language of Geography

The ability to understand and interpret symbols utilized in map study is the key to unlocking the language of geography. Naturally, in the primary grades, map materials should contain a limited number of symbols. Maps at this level are notable for their simplicity in lettering and use of color. Most children entering the kindergarten have had limited experience with maps. However, some youngsters will know that a map may indicate such things as part of the earth, rivers, highways, railroad lines and bridges. With this basic fund of knowledge, they can be led to further understanding of geographic concepts and map symbols.

Map Readiness

Imaginative map readiness experiences for children at the primary level are of the utmost necessity. One interesting technique is to have children prepare a simple map of the classroom. The teacher draws a demonstration map on the chalkboard, with the principles of direction and proportion clearly explained. Teach the children how lines and small sketches of physical objects are necessary symbols; they must be made to realize that objects cannot be drawn to their true size. They will see how any physical object can be included on many kinds of maps. Later, after completing several simple classroom maps, have them prepare floor plans of the school building, while constantly reminding them of the principles of scale and direction.

One idea is to encourage the group to draw a neighborhood map on either the class blackboard or bulletin board, using school mural paper or brown wrapping paper (Wrigley Map, Figure 8-4). The first step in such an activity is to tape a grid of all the streets on poster paper and letter their names on small pieces of colored construction paper. Next, have every child draw a simple sketch of their home and place it in its proper position on the map. In creating the map, children begin to learn the locations of such community services as the police and fire departments, post office and library.

Sandbox Map Fun

Let us not overlook one device for teaching map skills that is often available in primary classrooms and certainly kindergarten—a sandbox!

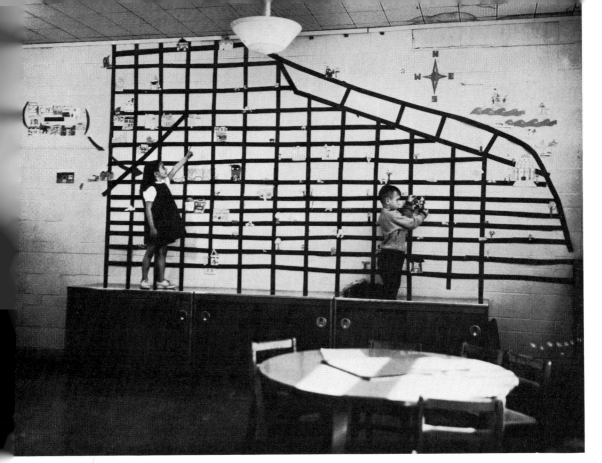

Figure 8-4

The Big Neighborhood Map

Ask the class to decide what areas they wish to map. Special land features can easily be molded in sand and made to hold their shape by spraying with a fine mist from a laundry sprinkler or similar device. Lakes and other bodies of water can be represented by mirrors or pieces of aluminum foil. Ordinary items, such as construction paper, colored strips of cloth, yarn and ribbon, will serve as a practical network of streams and rivers. Scrap blocks of wood from dad's or the custodian's workshop could make a fine stand-in for homes and important buildings.

The Reliable Road Map

Children at the intermediate level, being more mature in their work and study habits, are ready to deal with the more sophisticated map concepts and symbols. One of the most important map skills at the intermediate level is in developing the ability to read and interpret road maps. An amazing amount of learning can emanate from activities based on this type of map. State road maps are the best form for classroom exercises; however, they should be of uniform type. For this reason, it is wise

129

to secure enough copies from one of the large gasoline companies, rather than from the local service station. State road maps can also be obtained from state tourist bureaus. If a full-sized map of the United States is to be used, again the services of major oil companies should be called upon.

Road maps have a symbol indicating the four major directions. Show how to "orient" the map by placing it on a table, the floor, ground, or one's lap, with "N" to the North. Another feature is a marginal index which lists towns and cities by letter-number or decimal designation. The pupil learns to locate by finding the grid coordinates. Military personnel are taught, "Read Right Up"—go from left to right and then up—this makes for uniformity in designating and locating coordinates.

A multitude of exercises can be based on tracing road map routes. Crayons or grease pencils, or colored Magic Markers, are most effective in marking routes. Let's not forget that road maps show features like lakes, rivers and other works of nature and man. The children can also be introduced to the map scale, another reason for all having the same type of map.

Maps—Background for History

Maps can also act as springboards in fostering interest in history. Procure maps of a state with which the children have had some background, and guide them to spots that are historically important. All states are rich in historical heritage. The teacher and pupils who have visited historic shrines in any state could list these places on the chalkboard. Ask individual pupils to find the places on a wall map. After locating these historically famous sites, the teacher could have the class embark on a program of research to determine why each of these towns and cities became so important to the history of our country. Eventually, from an unpretentious road map, many learning experiences will be provided in written language, history, geography, reading and even math.

Make Your Own Symbol Map

The creation of a symbol map appeals readily to children at the intermediate level. The apperceptive background should include extensive experience in comparing photographs with map representations.

Place a legend for the symbol map on a bulletin board, chart or chalkboard. Symbols should be simple ones, such as those for a house, schoolhouse, church, or hills, marshes, lakes, wood, trails, railroads and orchards. Draw a sample of a symbol map, making certain to incorporate a number of the symbols from the symbol chart. The next procedure would be to have the children create their own map of their community or town. Also, they should be encouraged to experiment in laying out a mythical town. An amusing sidelight to this learning exercise can be to have the pupils name their town after themselves or a friend; e.g., *Mary*ville or *William*sport.

PRIMARY MAP ACTIVITIES

A Trip Around the Community   A community tour may be a walk or riding experience, depending on the distance from the school to the community. Before taking the trip, it would be advisable to secure a township map of your community. If the school bus is used, it would be wise to ask the driver to trace the routes in color. Route tracing should, of course, begin at the school. The next step is to have the children identify various properties as the bus comes to them. During route tracing, pupils will be able to learn directions, increase their vocabulary and finally, have a better understanding of map legends.

Pupil-Made Jigsaw Puzzles   Another device involves having the children trace or draw a map of a country or continent on a thin but stiff piece of cardboard. Then have the children cut their maps into interesting segments and shapes for the purpose of creating a jigsaw puzzle.

Relief Maps   Simple relief maps can also be attempted in primary grades; the easiest type is made with modeling clay. The outline of the object to be modeled should be placed on a stiff cardboard or plywood surface. The outline of a country may be lifted from a textbook, or other source by means of tracing paper, or transposed via the opaque or overhead projector. Once the map subject is transferred to the hard surface, the outline can be made more legible by going over it with a felt pen or similar marking device. Now surface features such as mountains and rivers may be added by shaping the model in clay as desired. Colored clay will add interest to the project.

Location Game   One interesting teaching procedure with the globe is to have one child call on another pupil to locate within a one-minute time limit some foreign country or geographic feature. If the student finds the country within the time period, he scores a point. The game can be played between two persons, or the class divided into teams.

INTERMEDIATE MAP ACTIVITIES

Shape of Things   Have the children study a specific area shown first on a globe, then on a flat map. Ask pupils to point to the four principal directions on both the globe and map. Explain carefully, and demonstrate with an hollowed out orange, what happens to the shape of the orange when it is flattened. A demonstration of this kind shows the distortions in the shape of continents that appear when we attempt to transfer images from a globe to a flat map.

Map Graphics Photographs of interesting land features, culled from magazines and newspapers that depict items such as mountains and lakes, can be successfully employed in helping children see the relationship between map symbols and the actual features they represent. Another idea with photographs is to have the children study a picture, as e.g., a hillside or a lake, and draw a sketch of what they have viewed. Sketches can then be compared to actual map symbols.

Map Scrapbook A map scrapbook can be a pleasurable and informative learning additive. Depending on the grade level, select a country or state, and have the children draw or copy an outline map on the first page of the scrapbook. On the succeeding pages, include drawings and newspaper or magazine clippings about the history, industries or customs of the particular state under study.

Let's Find Out! Children are often amazed when they learn that many flowers, vegetables and fruits had their origins in other parts of the world. With the help of the school librarian, assign pupils flowers, vegetables, or fruits, and have them research each item thoroughly. After the research is completed, have pupils indicate from what part of the world their assigned object came.

Geographic Mystery Clues Make up an assorted set of geographical clues, on 3 x 5″ cards, about well-known physical features and places, and have the pupils practice finding them on the globe.

Circling the Earth Place a globe on a table and superimpose thereon a small model boat. Make believe the boat is sailing on the ocean. Show the class how the boat vanishes from view as it circles the globe. Discuss the length of time it takes to sail to different points on the globe as compared to air travel.

Maps vs. Globes Here is an idea to show comparative sizes of countries and continents on the globe: Use tracing paper and copy an outline of the continent or country from the globe; then place this outline directly over another geographical area for comparison.

OPAQUE AND OVERHEAD PROJECTION

The Opaque—Helpful Art Assistant

The opaque projector is an always willing instructional servant in the primary and intermediate level of the social studies program. Almost everyone is aware that the opaque projector may be employed to project all varieties of maps on the classroom screen; yet the opaque projector shines best in its role of assisting children in successfully transferring drawings and diagrams from books, magazines, and newspapers to poster paper or the chalkboard.

Learning Through Collecting

One obvious but always effective idea for all elementary levels is to request your pupils to bring in photographs and souvenirs that were collected during vacation trips and display them for the whole class via opaque projection. A related idea is having a pupil display on the opaque projector: letters, photographs and postcards from friends or relatives in another state or country.

Coin and stamp collections make good viewing material for social studies lessons. One word of caution, however: Make sure that stamps are securely attached with stamp hinges to a stiff paper surface; otherwise the projector's blower or fan could cause a catastrophe by blowing the stamps away.

Transparencies with the overhead projector have numerous applications to the social studies curriculum, particularly in developing geographical concepts. There are many outstanding commercially produced transparencies available for effective instruction in the teaching of map skills. There are distinct advantages in utilizing the commercial type of transparencies because they are extremely well-made and thoroughly researched. When time is at a premium, carefully selected commercial transparencies, imaginatively used, can be a great asset in geography instruction. Large companies manufacturing transparencies have certain technical resources to which the classroom teacher does not have access (Figure 8-5).

3M Current Events Program

An interesting innovation, in teaching current events through commercial transparencies, is the new 3M Visual Products *News Focus*

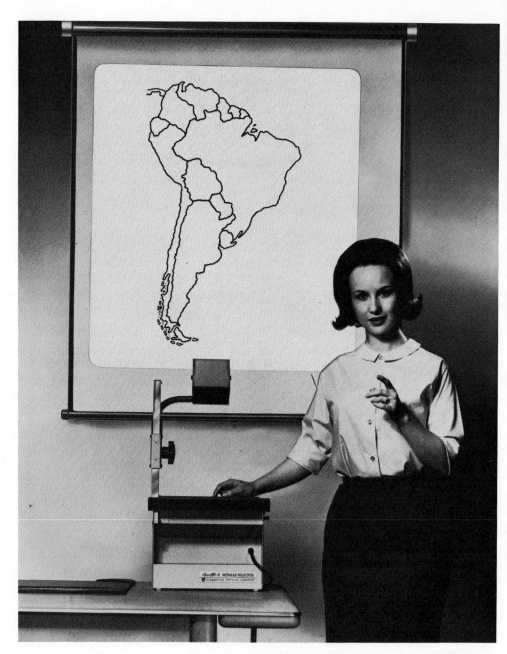

Figure 8-5

Map Study with the Overhead

program. This visual newsweekly is prepared by the editors of *Newsweek* and marketed by the 3M organization. Each issue of *News Focus* contains 8 x 10″ visuals that highlight the week's important news stories. These visuals, which consist of photos, diagrams, maps, graphs and cartoons, can be used for bulletin board display or easily transferred into a projection transparency. Every 3M visual has teaching suggestions for incorporation into lesson plans, as well as a comprehensive bibliography to assist teachers in securing additional information about news items.

There is also a definite place for student-prepared transparencies in social studies teaching. There are specific areas in the elementary school social studies curriculum that can only best be served by the non-commercial product; teacher and student-made transparencies are geared to current circumstances and not to a hypothetical instructional situation.

OPAQUE AND OVERHEAD PROJECTION ACTIVITIES

"Buzz Session"   Project on the opaque a series of pictures or illustrations dealing with such a subject as forest conservation or land erosion. Then have the class form into small groups of four to five persons, and invite them to have a "buzz session" about what they have viewed. Allow each group five to ten minutes to develop stimulating discussion and have the chairman of each tell about what they have viewed. This activity will probably work best at the intermediate level.

Individualized Map Research   Assign individual students textbook problems for preparing maps of the United States on highway systems or major waterways. Later, these maps can be converted into overhead transparencies for discussion purposes. Another related activity is to request that the class collect, from magazines and newspapers, photographs related to the particular area of geography they are studying. Ask each member of the class to show his collection; then select the best one for a series of projectuals.

War Campaign   Try to secure good map transparencies of some famous war campaign. A pertinent map will show the positions of the armies. Let individual pupils act as armchair generals, and ask them what strategy they would employ. After giving everyone this opportunity, discuss how the real battle was fought.

Fun and Politics   Make a copy of several transparencies of a political cartoon. Follow with class discussion on the significance and implication of various cartoons. Have the class make simple political cartoons of their own on drawing paper, chalkboard or acetate.

Time Line　Make a time line transparency. Let pupils use pertinent transparencies to illustrate their research reports and to motivate class discussion.

FILMSTRIPS, SLIDES, MOTION PICTURES AND TELEVISION

Filmstrips have much to recommend them for use in social studies lessons at all grade levels. They are, first of all, imaginative stimuli to introduce new social studies units. Second, they are an excellent pictorial tool for teaching map skills. Third, they serve as a dependable visual review device before a social studies quiz.

Ideal Field Trip Preparation

When planning a field trip to some nearby historic shrine or museum, it is advisable to show a filmstrip that is related to the subject matter the pupils will be seeing. If a class is scheduling a trip to a whaling museum, filmstrips dealing with these mammals or the regions where the whaling industry was prominent, would be just the thing.

Slides for Flexible Instruction

Color slides of picturesque land features, whether commercial or non-commercial, can make the geography lesson the highlight of the day. An imaginative set of slides or photographs of an historic landmark or restoration, such as Sturbridge Village or Colonial Williamsburg, can stimulate a lively social studies discussion period. Other visual aid material, such as souvenirs, postcards and other types of photographs, can supplement and augment the 2 x 2″ slides and give every youngster a thrilling glimpse into America's glorious past.

Most of the commercially-made slides that are based on specific topics are usually pre-arranged in a certain order. However, there is nothing to restrict a teacher from rearranging the sequence of slides or in combining certain individual slides to present an entirely different theme. Individually selected slides, for example, from sets on the Sahara Desert, Gobi Desert and the Great American Desert can be combined for a unit on hot, dry desert regions. Slides, whether taken by an amateur or a professional, become of inestimable value to social studies planning because of their inherent flexibility in arranging.

Value of 3¼ x 4″ Slides

The standard 3¼ x 4″ slide is extremely well-adapted to various aspects of social studies instruction. Maps, complicated charts, and diagrams generally show up better than the more modern 2 x 2″ slide transparencies. Copies of illustrations of land and water formations, weather, studies of life in other countries, and maps and charts on etched glass, are readily traced with pencil and colored with special crayons and ink.

The teacher can utilize typed cellophane slides. They are ideal for quizzes and copied text material. In history, pupil-made etched glass slides can illustrate historical characters and events, besides historical maps, graphs, and other pertinent data.

The Well-Made Social Studies Film

Many a social studies lesson is enhanced by the effective utilization of 16mm films on geography and history. At the primary level we have motion pictures dealing with community life, children in foreign lands, famous Americans, communication, transportation and democracy. At the intermediate level there are numerous films on world geography, world history, economics and map skills. The format of these movies varies: some are strictly pictorial reports, some are true drama enactment films and still other pictures are basically travelogues (Figures 8-6, 8-7 and 8-8).

During the course of the year, television's major networks offer exciting programs on famous people and specials based on newsworthy special events. Yet, unless it is a long-running series, it is almost impossible to enumerate in any textbook a list of current programs because of the tremendous program turnover from year to year.

Guidelines for Television

For ideas based on television specials, consult a good television guide, which should contain publicity on the particular program. If the program emanates from an educational television station and the school subscribes to its service, manuals should be available which contain many specific suggestions and activities for the program being telecast.

FILMSTRIPS, SLIDES, MOTION PICTURES
AND TELEVISION ACTIVITIES

Field Trip Correlation The filmstrip is a dependable device to use prior to a field trip and for a past field trip review. For example, a filmstrip on aviation could precede or follow up a field trip to an airport.

Paper Filmstrip Ask children to draw a paper strip based on se-

Courtesy Robert A. Fuller, CBS Publicity Department

Figure 8-6

Joan of Arc

Courtesy Robert A. Fuller, CBS Publicity Department

Figure 8-7

OK Corral

Courtesy of Coronet Instructional Films, Chicago, Ill.

Figure 8-8

Boy of Japan, Ito and His Kite

One excellent view of children in a foreign land.

quences shown in the filmstrip. Cut slits in white envelopes, through which the paper movie of the filmstrip may be pulled.

Filmstrip Reference Library   Send a committee of pupils to the school library to compile a bibliography on a listing of other library materials on a topic covered in a filmstrip.

Filmstrip and Slide Tableaux   Show filmstrips or 2 x 2″ slides depicting recent and significant historical events. Have pupil committees present historical tableaux based on the happenings shown in these visuals. Children may re-enact the events in the tableaux, such as the "Landing of the Pilgrims," "Columbus Discovering America" or more sophisticated material, depending on the circumstances.

Dual Slide Presentation   For an effective slide presentation, use two slide projectors and two portable screens to achieve a cineramic or panoramic visual effect. Pictures taken of the same historic building, historic site or scenic wonder, taken from different angles, provide a novel audio-visual approach to a social studies lesson. Pupils participate by assisting the teacher and selecting the best available commercial and non-commercial slides, and preparing supplementary and oral narratives accompanying the presentation.

Tourist Bureau Fun   Here is an idea that may generate a deeper interest in the study of our country and foreign lands. After showing one or a series of travel-oriented films, or travelog programs on television, have a group of students organize a fictitious travel bureau. Ask two or three pupils to take turns acting as the travel director, and have the remaining children in the group act as tourists. In this activity, have your pupil-travel director plan his make-believe tourist itinerary just as a real travel director would. If possible, prior to the scheduled showing of the travelog, plan a combined social studies-English exercise in which pupils write to professional travel bureaus and embassies of foreign countries for background information and travel posters.

BULLETIN BOARDS AND FLANNEL BOARDS

Ideas Unlimited for Bulletin Boards

There is never a shortage of subject matter themes for elementary school bulletin boards, and the social studies curriculum abounds with possible themes. Transportation, communication, industry, products, legacies from the past, United States history, and history and customs of foreign lands are just some of the topics that can inspire imaginative social studies display boards.

Attractive elementary bulletin boards should place their reliance on pupils' efforts. Likewise, they can be a careful blend of children's work and professional graphic materials. The bulletin board must be clear to the beholder and concentrate on a few aspects of one basic idea. Since most children's drawings and construction work can sometimes be highly cluttered or appear busy, the border designs and general arrangement of the bulletin board should be kept simple. This is particularly true of primary level bulletin boards. In addition, primary bulletin boards require a higher degree of teacher guidance.

Flannel Magic

Can we weave the spell of "flannel magic" in social studies? "Flannel magic" is a term often used by children to describe the wonders of the flannel board. The flannel board, or feltboard, is a truly versatile teaching device ideally suited for the presentation of factual material and concepts in history and geography. It is a visual device with built-in sight appeal.

Flannel boards for social studies purposes do not have to be elaborate or massive in size. For teaching large groups of children, an 18 x 28″ size is recommended and smaller flannel boards ranging from a 4 x 5″ to 8 x 11″ are suggested for individual use.

Handbooks that contain further ideas for teaching social studies are *Teaching with the Flannel Board* (The Instructo Corporation, Paoli, Pa. 19301) and *Felt Boards for Teaching* (University of Texas, Visual Instruction Bureau, Austin, Texas 78712). A noteworthy catalyst, to stimulating ideas for bulletin board projects, is the booklet "Social Studies Bulletin Boards" by Miriam Silcox, published by Teachers Publishing Corporation, Darien, Conn. 06820.

PRIMARY BULLETIN BOARD AND FLANNEL BOARD ACTIVITIES

A 3-Dimensional Supermarket Idea   Plan a bulletin board that consists of an outline or silhouette of a supermarket and then mount on the board actual empty cartons representing packages of products actually sold therein. They may be affixed by using products such as "bulletin board wax," Anchor-Dough or double-faced pressure-sensitive tape.

Down on the Farm Drawings   With the children, arrange a bulletin board that depicts a typical farm scene replete with a cutout barn, silo and farmhouse. Then lay out, in a well-balanced pattern, a series of their own drawings descriptive of farm life.

Indian Life Bulletin Board   Arrange on the display board an orderly display of magazine illustrations and pupils' drawings. At the base of the board that depicts Indian life, place a project table containing samples of such Indian cultural relics as pottery, dolls, and leather crafts.

Geographic Bulletin Boards   In a study of regional geography, use magazines, photographs, postcards and other illustrated materials for a bulletin board display. To make this a more unique learning experience, prepare a series of questions in which the illustrative material in itself actually answers the questions.

Big City—Rural Areas   Prepare a bulletin board on themes of the large city and rural areas. Use pictures cut from magazines or pupil drawings depicting big city life or life in a country setting.

Flannel Board Resource Map   A flannel board resource map can be made by first cutting out an outline of a state or country from flannel materials, or, if this is too difficult, by using a commercially prepared outline map backed with felt. Place this flannel silhouette or outline map of the state or country directly on your regular flannel board. Next, either cut from magazines or prepare simple sketches of food products or mineral resources that are representative of the state or country to be labeled. If neither pictures nor drawings are available, just print the name of the products on the card with a felt pen. Mount the drawings, magazine illustrations or printed card on flannel or some other sensitized backing material and have the children place the products on the appropriate location on the map.

INTERMEDIATE BULLETIN BOARD AND FLANNEL BOARD ACTIVITIES

Famous People   Make a bulletin board highlighting a famous person. Place a large magazine picture of the personality in a prominent position; then surround this picture with magazine articles, pictures and pupils' drawings, and compositions dealing with events in the personality's life.

Flags, Stamps and Coins of Foreign Lands   Select a continent, and make a huge map of it via the opaque or film projector. Surround the map outline with flags and pupils' drawings, and stamp and coin collections. For obvious reasons, the stamps and coins should be enclosed in transparent plastic before being secured to the display board.

Symbols of American Patriotism   Prepare a bulletin board with patriotic quotations arranged in a marginal fashion. Complete the display with either drawings or magazine photography of patriotic symbols like the Liberty Bell, Uncle Sam and the Statue of Liberty, or arrange a montage of illustrations of historic shrines, such as Valley Forge and the Lincoln Memorial.

The Melting Pot Collect magazine pictures depicting ethnic groups that have migrated to America. A huge kettle silhouette could be used to show New York City as the "melting pot" of America. Show each ethnic group's contributions to America's culture.

Back into Time Employ the flannel board in teaching a unit on medieval history. Have pupils make drawings of medieval knights and ladies, serfs, castles and huts; then mount them on flannel material and place them on the flannel board. Interesting medieval towns or kingdoms can be realistically re-created in this imaginative visual medium.

Visualizing the Structure of Government A variation in the above activity is to use the flannel board to demonstrate how a bill becomes a law or to illustrate the structure of governments. In preparing flannel-backed cardboard cutouts for the class, make sure the side facing out is a smooth surface which can be printed on by either a Magic Marker, crayon or pen.

DIORAMAS

The diorama readily lends itself, in social studies instruction, to capturing the imagination and re-creating real life happenings and historical events.

Dynamic Diorama

A trip to a museum is perhaps the best way to acquaint your pupils with the values of dioramas. Museums have dioramas that are faithful and realistic reproductions of historic and geographic scenes and views from foreign lands. Some museums will often loan to schools a number of the portable dioramas designed by expert craftsmen. Such professionally constructed displays are worth a thousand teaching words.

Unless children have had extensive experience with dioramas, a certain background of knowledge must be made available to them, or it will be difficult for them to embark on ideas of their own. First of all, they must see different types of dioramas, both full-scale and miniature types. Try to procure a set of 2 x 2″ slides showing dioramas. Picture files of objects to be reproduced will also be helpful.

A Blueprint for Initiating Diorama Activities

It would be wise, when initiating your first diorama activity, to select one theme to dramatize rather than varied topics. There should be plenty of class discussion on the objectives of the diorama before pupils are asked to outline their plans. One of the initial planning steps should require each student to prepare a sketch of how he thinks the dioramic scene should look. Children, in making these preliminary sketches, will find that extensive research will be a necessity, before and after drawing their sketches, in order to insure the utmost accuracy

The sketch will serve as a guide to constructing the diorama. The teacher should go over with the class such points as the size of the diorama, what the background scenes should depict, and ways to create 3-dimensional images and achieve perspective.

Low-Cost Dioramas

Simple dioramas can be created out of old shoeboxes, wooden crates, cardboard cartons or hatboxes. A cylindrical hatbox naturally will make an ideal panoramic setting for a diorama. Our first step is to cut away the front of the hatbox. Next, a picturesque scene is sketched and colored on white drawing paper. This background or "scenery" may be affixed to the rear of the hatbox "stage" with staples, clips or glue. The stage may be populated with five- and ten-cent toy figures or inexpensive dolls placed in their predetermined locations.

Special Diorama Effects

Imaginative 3-dimensional objects may be devised from pipe cleaners, empty thread spools, soap-carved figures and wood-carved figures. People may be constructed from figures drawn on paper, then mounted on cardboard. These cardboard figures may be placed in a wooden block base that has a slit cut in it; the slit will allow the cardboard object to stay upright.

Landscaping features can be simulated by using a cardboard box covered over with chicken wire. Plaster of Paris or layers of papier-maché may be poured over the wire surface. This covering, when thoroughly dried, may be painted. Grass can be colored sawdust; dyed twigs, sponge and pine cones may serve as shrubs and trees; wood match sticks with string will serve well as telephone lines; toothpicks carefully laid out will make an excellent railroad track; scrap pieces of wood easily secured from the lumber yard and painted will be fine buildings. Toy trucks and cars shouldn't be hard to locate.

Other Diorama Effects

Colored cellophane can be used to good effect on many dioramas. Green cellophane will make a forest or jungle scene more realistic. Blue cellophane will dramatize an underwater scene. Yellow cellophane will make a hot desert scene more intense.

Even objects like ships, such as the Vikings' or Columbus', are easy to construct for dioramas. The first step is to bind two shoeboxes to form the hull of the ship. The shoeboxes are covered with several layers of papier-maché. Masts of the ship may be wooden dowels or perhaps an old curtain rod. The dowel or cardboard cylinders are inserted in the hull of the ship and then covered with two to three layers of maché. Now paint the hull and ship's mast and attach. Allow the painted hull and mast to dry, before attaching masts, made of white construction paper.

An interesting teaching aid, containing projects and useful teaching suggestions for social studies purposes at the intermediate level, is the "Handbook of Instructional Devices," by Sondra Waltz, published by Teachers Publishing Corporation, Darien, Conn. 06820.

Social Studies Fair

When children are sufficiently experienced in constructing dioramas and models, why not plan a social studies exhibition or fair of their work? Remember, exhibits consist not only of dioramas and models, but also flat pictures, posters and other displays. Appropriate records, tape recordings and filmstrips dealing with social studies themes, could serve as an imaginative backdrop to the fair. Pupil-made posters, murals and time-line charts should be an integral part of the exhibit.

IDEAS FOR DIORAMAS

A Pioneer's Life   Construct a diorama showing the interiors of pioneer homes, churches, schools and general stores. Accompany each diorama with a short report on what the diorama is depicting.

Medieval Castle   An interesting diorama activity is the creation of a medieval castle. Make this a group activity having different youngsters who worked on the project explain each feature of the castle orally to the rest of the class.

Historical Community   After collecting material on famous historic restorations, such as Colonial Williamsburg, make a series of dioramas showing easily reproduced sections of this historical community.

The Peep Box   A novel type of diorama and one which contains an element of mystery (which is sure to appeal to the imagination and curiosity of the class) is a peep box. Actually, a social studies peep box is nothing more than a diorama based on some historical event or geographical setting, but the front of the diorama is covered with an opaque cardboard screen. A large enough peephole is cut out in the cardboard screen, thus allowing curious viewers to take a peep at the show inside. Arrangements should be made to form small committees of individual pupils to construct the peepshow dioramas in complete secrecy. The teacher may recommend that the children do these projects at home to insure this element of secrecy. This is an area in which the classroom teacher can decide how this activity can be best carried out.

SUMMARY

The implements of audio-visual media relate themselves readily to practically all areas in the elementary social studies curriculum. The subject matter of social studies in itself has a built-in appeal, and audio-visual materials, when used with imagination, can effectively capitalize on this attraction.

9

GETTING
MORE FROM
AUDIO-VISUAL AIDS IN
TEACHING MUSIC

The climate for effective learning in music must be truly permissive, creative and pliable. Teachers should break with many of the present-day regimented and highly structured instructional patterns. As in science, children must learn from discovery, imagination and experimentation.

One of the most valuable keys to music instruction is the tape recorder. It can be creatively employed to teach rhythm and harmony, to introduce new songs, to practice and evaluate. The disc recording has long been a reliable standby for teaching music appreciation for several decades, and now it expands its use to include teaching folk dances and encouraging amateur rhythm orchestras. Certainly, radio can exert a strong influence in music instruction. A twist of the AM or FM dial can bring a variety of all types of music into our classroom, ranging from opera to classical, and from semi-classical and folk music to, yes, even rock and roll!

Two of the most productive visuals in music are the opaque and the overhead projector. The overhead, in particular, can more imaginatively and efficiently show what is usually written on the chalkboard: namely, music symbols. Most important, the overhead projects a large enough image that both small and large audiences can readily view the projectual.

The sound tracks of motion pictures, often unheralded by critics as an intrinsic reason behind many film successes, are ideal for purposes of music appreciation and class discussion. Many of the virtues cited for motion pictures may be added to television's undeniable plus, the element of immediacy.

The media of display, namely the bulletin board, flannel board and realia, provide the music instructor with a wide assemblage of teaching materials that will assist him in providing long-lasting visual impressions. There seems to be an increasing interest by teachers in encouraging pupils to make their own simple instruments, thus adding another magical ingredient for learning music—self participation.

AUDIO TEACHING TECHNIQUES

The skill of listening, so strongly emphasized in our language arts instruction, is an integral part of the scheme of things in our music curriculum.

Become Musical Explorers

In the primary grades, appreciation of music is engendered by phonograph records. Records allow the young pupil to become exposed to a wide range of musical experiences, enabling the imaginative student to become a musical explorer. Recordings are a focal point or background for pupil-singing activities.

When a pupil reaches the intermediate level in school he becomes more concerned with the mechanics of music form, style, interpretation and symbols, and the cultural background and heritage of music. Records are a valuable means to teach the fundamentals of music and its historical legacy.

Most record companies, being aware of the role of listener participation in music, are producing improved aural aids. Bowmar Records, Inc. of Glendale, California, has a comprehensive record library collection available including, "Meet the Instruments," "Rhythm Time," "Folk Songs of the U.S.A.," "Holiday Songs," "Songs from Singing Fun," etc. Likewise, producers like Folkways/Scholastic, 50 West 44th St., New York, N.Y. 10036 and American Book Company, 55 Fifth Avenue, New York, N.Y. 10003, frequently circulate engrossing record albums that can be fitted to a music teacher's instructional format (Figures 9-1 and 9-2).

We've Got Rhythm

Rhythm records are a good introduction to music appreciation and listening skills, and they develop a greater sense of critical listening. Records of this nature enable pupils to readily distinguish different tempos. Later, when a pupil begins to master different rhythm instru-

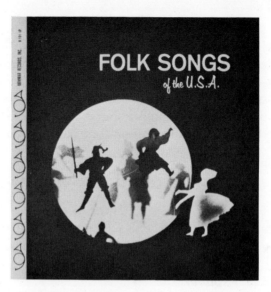

"By permission of the copyright owner, Bowmar Records, Inc., Glendale, California."

Figure 9-1

"Folk Songs from the U.S.A."

"By permission of the copyright owner, Bowmar Records, Inc., Glendale, California."

Figure 9-2

"Songs from Singing Fun"

Bowmar Records, Inc., offers imaginative record series ideal for music activities with elementary grade children.

ments, the teacher is free to employ the record a second or third time, with various combinations of instruments. This technique can pave the way for the formation of class rhythm bands.

Musical recordings can acquaint pupils with the great composers of the past and present. The name of the composer will be meaningless to the student unless he associates the music with the artist. After listening to a recording that is representative of the composer, it is interesting to get pupils' reactions to that particular musical selection.

A study of how musical forms maintain their character through the passage of time can be accomplished through appropriate classical recordings that illustrate a certain type of music. Recordings that highlight certain instruments could lead to an in-depth study of the characteristics of that instrument.

Courtesy of RCA Victor Records, New York, N.Y.

Figure 9-3

Adventures in Music. Grade 1 Photo Album

Music becomes exciting with the record library series such as RCA's "Adventures in Music" for elementary schools.

Courtesy of RCA Victor Records, New York, N.Y.

Figure 9-4

Adventures in Music. Grade 2 Photo Album

Music becomes exciting with the record library series such as RCA's "Adventures in Music" for elementary schools.

Now Is the Time for Musical Pantomime

Pantomime and puppetry can be combined with music, effecting important learning benefits. Classical mood music such as Prokofieff's "Children's Suite-Waltz on the Ice," Saint Saëns "Carnival of Animals," Mc Donald's "Children's Symphony," Grieg's "In the Hall of the Mountain King" and Tchaikovsky's "Nutcracker Suite" can be the nucleus of unlimited creative pantomime and puppet exercises. The splendid RCA "Adventures in Music" is a ten-record series which has graded musical selections and includes many of the aforementioned compositions (Grade 1 sample, Figure 9-3; Grade 2 sample, Figure 9-4).

The geography and culture of a country are certainly influential in the music of a nation and its people. An interesting exercise is to present authentic folk music and contrast it to modern music—and the best way to do this is through recordings.

The Audio Handy Man

The tape recorder can be a music teacher's handy man in demonstrating two, three or four-part harmony. The first step is to familiarize the class thoroughly with the song, then let the group tape it. Later, the class may be taught the harmonizing parts, and when this has been accomplished, it may be sung.

The tape recorder is invaluable for pupils who are learning an instrument to check their timing and tonal balances. The recorder allows pupils to evaluate their singing and instrumental performances on tape playbacks. Furthermore, music on tape enables pupils in an elementary band to drill more effectively in marching. It is also ideal at orchestra, choir, band or chorus rehearsals where various sections may learn how to recognize their cues.

The tape recorder is also ideal for assembly programs and outdoor festivals, because it is an excellent stand-in musical accompanist, if the scheduled performer might not be available. As a dependable aid for teachers who are not endowed with musical skill, taped piano passages make fine audio backdrops for primary level music participation activities.

Music in the Air

AM and FM radio both have extensive radio programming with decided emphasis on music. Where educational FM is available, most of these facilities furnish manuals with suggested teaching techniques and activities. Foreign language stations usually feature music indigenous to the country and are a noteworthy source for authentic music of the land and its people. Generally, music programming is so well-balanced, a study of newspaper listings for the day will bring any kind of music whenever desired.

AUDIO ACTIVITIES

The Musical Keys to the Past   Have pupils study a certain historical personality like George Washington and research the kind of music that was in vogue in the period with which he was associated.

Sight and Sound   Ask pupils to bring to class illustrations from old magazines that represent a certain mood or setting. Utilize the school record library as a source for auditioning a series of records until a recording is found that will aurally match or capture the essence of the visual.

Stop the Music!   Put the traditional musical quiz in the format of the old radio and TV "Stop the Music" favorite. In the classroom suspend two bells down to a child's height. On the floor, a starting place can be marked, using masking tape or chalk to indicate the starting point where two contestants are lined up. Select two pupil contestants to enter in the competition, guessing the identity of various musical passages being played on the phonograph record. The contestant who recognizes the tune runs toward the bell and rings it. If the contestant sounds the bell, but doesn't correctly name the tune, no point is scored. If both contestants know the selection, the one who first rings the bell and correctly names the tune is declared the winner.

Music Maestro Please   Try to show films or filmstrips that demonstrate how a conductor leads his musicians and show the class all the gestures that a conductor would employ. Later, select a series of recordings appropriate to children's ages and interest levels, and have individual pupils act as guest conductors and pantomime the concert master leading an imaginary orchestra via the recording.

Disc Jockey   Have pupils make believe they are radio disc jockeys who must come up with a program of appropriate music to fit a certain theme. Pupils could prepare listings based on folk tunes, operas, classical and semi-classical music. Musical selections appropriate to certain holidays and occasions, such as Christmas or St. Patrick's Day, should appeal to most children. After the planning is completed, encourage children to simulate an actual radio program replete with even commercials and comments.

Sounds from Which to Compose Music Play a recording of various sounds from around the home, or a series of unrelated sound effects. Encourage pupils to invent a simple melody that these sound effects inspire. Older pupils, familiar with the symbols of music, may wish to write music and even words to fit their creative compositions. The Folkways/Scholastic Records' "Milions of Musicians" and "New York 19," which are collections of environmental sounds, serve as an imaginative introduction to this activity, since they demonstrate how these environmental sounds generally make a music of their own.

Sing-Along Time Combine recordings of non-vocal musical selections with the tape recorder. Ask pupil volunteers to sing the words of a familiar tune along with the recording, and tape the music on the spot. Later, play the tape back and see how our vocalists sound.

VISUAL TECHNIQUES

The opaque projector is relied upon heavily for a magnified reproduction of words and lyrics from a music book. Furthermore, illustrative material, namely photographs of famous composers or any type of visual illustrating a certain sequence of music, can be projected.

A majority of music teachers will find that the overhead is the most valuable of all projected visuals. Its main value stems from the fact that it is a time-saver, since lessons can be readily put on transparencies, hours or even days in advance without all the effort involved in writing on the chalkboard.

Words and Music by . . .

Most overhead projectors come equipped with a roll of acetate. It is very easy to copy down the musical score and lyrics on the acetate roll. A simple cartoon might supply an additional dash of humor and interest to the music being inscribed. As you turn the roll of acetate, plan to accompany the projectual with recordings of the music. The audio combined with the overhead visual can add much to the music lesson. A pencil will make a perfect pointer while the music is being studied on the screen.

Band directors and chorus instructors are discovering that transparencies can be used to show choral seating arrangements and to illustrate marching patterns for the band.

The Right Note for Music

Most teachers would rely on charts and textual materials to acquaint pupils with musical notation. However, reliance on these materials creates problems. The big handicap is that once a text is in the hands of pupils, the teacher finds it difficult to persuade the student to concentrate on specific details of notation. Charts, especially large ones, create difficulty since they are not as durable as smaller ones. Since children are more exposed to printed words early in their schooling, their attention is obviously going to be confined to mastering only the lyrics. A series of transparencies that show musical notations without the distraction of words will assist the instructor in speeding up this phase of musical learning.

By utilizing the techniques of hinged overlays (which are merely transparent acetate sheets attached like pages in a book) musical notation can be taught in controlled stages. For example, a series of three overlapping transparencies could show a treble clef, base clef, and finally, the lyrics of a musical composition; thus the teacher is the master of the lesson because pupils are not being distracted by too much material being shown at one sitting.

There are transparencies for large class instruction that illustrate correct fingering movements of instruments such as the flutephone or recorder. A comprehensive, commercially-prepared music instructive series devised by Merrill Debski is available from Tecnifax/Viscom, 20 First Ave., Chicopee, Mass. 01020. These commercially-prepared visuals of the musical staffs have the lines of these staffs indelibly inscribed in the acetate so that they will remain after the grease pencil marks are wiped off. This also permits pupils to do class and homework assignments directly on the acetate itself. Such flexibility would not be available with ordinary textbook instruction.

Filmstrip manufacturers are producing some attractive series. For example, SVE (Society for Visual Education, Inc.) 1343 Diversey Pkwy., Chicago, Ill. 60614, is distributing correlated filmstrip record sets which include "Our Heritage of American Folk Music," "Christmas Songs in Foreign Languages" and "Developing Skills in Music." The Jam Handy Organization of Detroit, Michigan, has six color filmstrips based on the life stories of such famed composers as Bach, Handel, Haydn, etc. Eye Gate House, Inc., 146-01 Archer Ave., Jamaica, N.Y. 11435, has produced a combination filmstrip and $33\frac{1}{3}$ LP presentation on the theory, terminology and symbolism of music, specially designed for elementary classrooms, entitled "Let's Learn about Music" and "It's Fun to Read Music."

Tammy!

A number of years ago an unheralded movie, "Tammy" starring Debbie Reynolds, became a mild sensation at the box office—which is really an amazing paradox since the film was not acclaimed for its artistic merits or the popularity of the star. The reason for the film's success was directly attributed to its theme song, "Tammy." (Interestingly enough, when the film was first released, no one paid much attention, but with the increasing popularity of the song, the movie was re-released and became a financial success.) This substantiates the fact that a music sound track is a highly influential force in the field of motion pictures and can be an effective instructional aid. Interesting lessons can be based on the theory that music in motion pictures and television helps establish moods of happiness, sorrow, fright and anger.

Pupils can be requested to watch specific musical programs, usually television specials such as operas, Broadway musicals and young people's concerts. Music will be more meaningful when associated with a pupil's environment—and certainly, television is part of a child's environment.

VISUAL ACTIVITIES

I Hear Music Run a film that the class has never seen, with the projection lamp off, but with the sound track on. Discuss with the class what they thought was taking place during these musical interludes. Later show the film with picture and sound, and encourage comments from the pupils about the effective role of music to stimulate emotion.

Let's Compose a Tune This activity is variable enough to encourage pupils who have a good sense of rhythm and musical appreciation, to compose simple melodies. The class can be divided into two committees. One group might write, individually or collectively, a transparency of their own scores, while the other group tries to match lyrics to melodies.

Illustrative Musical Terms The teacher can prepare a transparency that lists a number of musical terms which can be visibly represented by a drawn symbol on the transparency itself or on the chalkboard.

A Film Musical Make a short 8mm or 16mm color film based on changing seasons, weather, animal life or school activities. After the film is processed and shown to the class, try to elicit from pupils suggestions on the type of recorded music that will complement the picture.

Musical Notation Separate the class into two teams. Use a transparency that illustrates musical notations and ask questions about the notes on the musical staff. If the pupil answers accurately, continue the question until someone misses. After a miss, the opposing team is queried. The two groups can be patterned after basketball, baseball or football teams, with a point scoring system devised.

DISPLAY TECHNIQUES

Musical Heritage of Days Gone by

There are many ways to teach music through displays. The ever-reliable bulletin board is the better vehicle to promote interest in music. Many themes for bulletin boards can be based on America's historical past. Songs of different eras and musical contributions of various ethnic groups can capture the spirit of the period and people. The social studies curriculum and music programs can be imaginatively combined on the bulletin board. Songs like "Wait for the Wagon," "Tenting Tonight" or "Swanee River" can be the inspiration for historically-oriented music bulletin boards.

The flannel board is well suited in the primary grades to help pupils learn harmony as well as counterpoint and to acquaint them with notes and note values. Commercially-produced flannel sets have kits with a felt backdrop and provide flannel cutouts of flats, charts, notes, rests and clef signs for this type of instruction. As with the overhead, band formation can be visualized by arranging felt discs on the board in various patterns. Music flow charts, to illustrate certain procedures, points and relationships, can be easily made on oaktag backed with appropriate sensitized material, with terms to be printed with a felt marker.

So You Want to Lead a Band

The new trend in creative music instruction is to have pupils use simple and inexpensive instruments to make music more pleasurable. Some teachers are showing children how to make their own instruments. Techniques for constructing the instruments may be found in *Making and Playing Classroom Instruments,* published by Fearon, San Francisco, California, and Martha Rosenberg's *It's Fun to Teach Creative Music,* published by Play Schools Association, New York.

DISPLAY ACTIVITIES

Composer's Corner Set up a classroom bulletin board around the life and music of a famous composer. Magazine illustrations, pupil-drawings, and research reports concerned with the author's background and accomplishments, are a good starting point.

Musical Art Use such symbols of music as sharps, flats and clef signs as the basis for fascinating abstract patterns. Colored crayons will make this form of musical art visualization more pleasing to the eye.

MacNamara's Band   For truly creative music, have pupils make their own versions of professional instruments. Soda bottles, or glasses filled with varying amounts of water and struck carefully, will not sound like the xylophone in the New York Philharmonic Orchestra, but such instruments will make music fun. Drums never cease to intrigue youngsters and they can be developed from commonplace objects such as boxes, coffee cans, plastic and galvanized pails, and hat boxes. These basic materials, when carefully prepared, make excellent drums that produce satisfactory sound. The ends of the coffee can or beach pail must be covered by material such as parchment paper or cloth, stretched across the top of the container. Twine and strong cord can be used to secure the covering and keep it adjusted (see artist's drawing, Figure 9-5).

Illustration by Cathy Johnson

Figure 9-5
MacNamara's Band

Maracas are also easy to prepare. All you need is a jar, tin can or cardboard box, although any type of closed container will suffice. Pour material like dried beans or gravel into the container and shake. Other ingredients that make intriguing maracas sound effects are paper clips, rice, tacks or screws. Gongs can be fashioned from old car hub caps or garbage can lids. Since gongs must have resonance, the best improvised gongs are items made from steel or brass.

MUSICAL PROGRAMS

Play acting has always been a fascinating experience for children, and musical plays are doubly exciting. It is not difficult to put on a musical assembly program; most of the songs and dances can be drawn from the music curriculum, the themes selected from social studies. Reading dramatic techniques are drawn from language arts.

The first step in developing a musical play is to appraise your pupils' singing and dancing talents. Simple costumes can be made by the pupils from inexpensive crepe paper or dyed muslin. Parental assistance in costuming is always welcome. Two excellent sources for costume making are the booklets "Creative Costumes," published by F. A. Owen of Dansville, New York and "Easy-To-Make Colorful Costumes," published by the Teaching Publishing Corporation of Darien, Connecticut, which contain directions for making costumes for fairy tales, historical stories and folklore.

It is a wise rule in planning a musical program to build up a resource file of musical ideas, including songs and dances, and above all, keep an eye out for children who have any special musical and dramatic abilities, and keep them in mind when you are casting parts in the production.

In choosing themes for the musical program, try to settle on one subject of universal interest to children, rich in dramatic appeal, and a theme which lends itself to musical enrichment. Some ideal topics, which are dramatically attractive and rich in musical resources, are: historical events, folk music, the seasons and holidays.

At the intermediate level, committees can be formed to produce manuscripts. A good idea is to have pupils put on an impromptu or spontaneous pantomime or skit in which pupils imagine themselves in specific situations and speak extemporaneously without the restriction of formal script. By performing in an informal way, children develop an ability to speak naturally and learn to act in a relaxed manner. Deriving a script by recording the spontaneous dialogue of the impromptu dramatizations is an ideal way to utilize audio-visual techniques in the creation of an original play.

Children who are selected for speaking parts should receive credit for them by reading a narrative before the entire class. Those who are chosen should be selected on the basis of pronunciation and diction.

The dramatic phase of the program should be rehearsed separately from the musical portion during the first few weeks of practice. Later, both the dramatic phase and music portions are brought together for full rehearsal.

During the weeks of rehearsal the committee of pupils, with the teacher's guidance, can be working on scenery and costumes. Music in the context of the class play makes music serve a purpose, and in doing so, music becomes more meaningful. As with any subject, it is important to relate the special field of learning to a child's environment.

SUMMARY

New trails must be blazed in musical instruction. The old must be blended with the new. The old paths of instruction have been trod too often and are well-worn, and the music specialist must necessarily employ innovative techniques, spiced with imaginative audio-visual aids, so that their captive pupil audience will look upon learning music as a truly pleasurable thing.

In this chapter we have seen that disc recordings can be employed to instruct children in learning harmony and rhythm at the primary level. Both the novice and experienced teacher can depend upon today's disc recordings for a rich array of creative activities which can develop a deep appreciation of music at an early age. In addition, the tape recorder remains an attractive aural musical drillmaster and helps the music teacher preserve music on a more permanent basis.

The opaque and overhead projectors can, individually or in concert with one another, visually demonstrate musical notation with more telling effect than perhaps exclusive reliance on the traditional chalkboard medium. Moreover, plain inexpensive acetates for pupil use provide practice in what he has been taught in the music class. Sometimes the simple things in life are best, and perhaps simply-made pupil instruments, which will call for active student involvement, will encourage children at a much earlier age to enter the world of music.

10

NEW
AUDIO-VISUAL PATTERNS
FOR MORE EFFECTIVE
ART INSTRUCTION

The emphasis on audio-visual aids in art instruction is primarily on the visual and display media. Both opaque and overhead projectors can stimulate interest in art of the past, give insight into the techniques of art, and bring about a realization that the world of art surrounds us daily. Commercial filmstrips too are making art appreciation meaningful, and many arts and crafts filmstrips are systematically demonstrating to pupils the various techniques involved in art activities. Motion pictures and television are practical ways to show pupils art being put to work and to place art in a meaningful relationship with reality.

When we think of art, we usually don't think of textbooks. But, there are many excellent well illustrated books on the market for classroom use. Most publishers of art books are devising formats that allow for flexibility in teaching, with reflections on the latest theories and developments in art instruction.

Four excellent handbooks containing creative ideas and information, helpful for long-range planning in the art curriculum, are the 48-page "Your Art Idea Book," "Scrap Craft," "Easy-to-Makes" and "Art Magic," published by F. A. Owen Publishing Co., Instructor Park, Dansville, N.Y. 14437.

Many classroom teachers look to art teachers for new and imaginative bulletin boards. It is not in the least unusual for art teachers to use the bulletin board for their own instruction. It still remains one of the most inexpensive means to communicate with the class, the only major requirements being time and planning. Unlike bulletin boards, the flannel board and chalkboard also facilitate art instruction, but they require less pre-planning and very little preparation time; thus, it is extremely important to employ novel materials in unique ways and utilize common materials in an uncommon manner.

PROJECTED MATERIALS

The Art Appreciation Way

Art teachers are constantly trying to instill in pupils a lasting appreciation for art. This means exhibiting to the class samples of color harmony and good design. By using clippings cut from old magazines and Sunday's color-photo sections, excellent and inexpensive visuals are available to bring out qualities of artistic design and color balance.

The opaque is just the right vehicle for doing stage scenery and making classroom murals because it readily projects a magnified image on canvas, flats or backdrops, or bulletin board paper.

Don't Be Vague—Use the Opaque

Pupils' art work can be analyzed and studied by their teacher and classmates by utilization of the opaque (Figure 10-1). It is also the ideal device to enable the viewer to study reproductions of old masters. Selected pages from expensive art books can be projected and appreciated for all to view and discuss. Color reproductions which are printed on glossy paper seem to sparkle under the intensity of the projector's light.

The opaque is an ideal means of training pupils to recognize examples of good architecture and sculpture as well as to identify famous paintings. The group, after exposure to art masterpieces, may be tested on the ability to recall each master.

Imaginative Overhead Ideas

The art teacher can show the technique for modeling clay right on an overhead projector's stage. Pupils in both the back and front of the room will be able to view the manipulation by watching the changing outline of the clay. By employing a series of transparent overlays, the teacher can demonstrate the various steps in drawing the human figure, with attention directed to distinguishing major body areas and facial characteristics.

The implements of art media can be viewed by means of the overhead. Of course, many of these articles, because they are not transparent, will project an opaque image. However, different paint brushes can be projected on the overhead so that pupils can see the variations in shape, size and texture.

The Complete Visual—the Filmstrip

Each nation, ancient and modern, has made some contribution to the world of art. A study of specific cultures in social studies, leading to an analysis of that civilization's contribution, could serve as the basis of an art filmstrip appreciation lesson.

Filmstrips based on the methods of art can be utilized as introduction to pertinent art techniques. Specific steps in art techniques can be studied in detail and the filmstrip of this nature can always be employed as a refresher or review. Of course, any filmstrip dealing with any subject area can be analyzed and judged for artistic qualities and color effectiveness by either teacher or pupil.

Figure 10-1

Analyzing Pupils' Art Work

Courtesy of Charles Beseler, East Orange, N.J.

While there is no overabundance of filmstrip titles for specific art purposes, the ones that are available are certain to be of value for art appreciation and instruction. The Society of Visual Education (1345 Diversey Parkway, Chicago, Illinois 60614) has produced "Art Activities for Primary Grades," a filmstrip which touches on such topics as mosaics, printmaking, hand puppets, collage and resist techniques. For instruction with older pupils, "Art Activities for Middle Grades" covers such areas as projected design, potato printing and sculpturing. SVE also has an intriguing color filmstrip series entitled "Holiday Art Activities."

Eye Gate House, Jamaica, N.Y. has a set of color filmstrips, "Artists of Many Lands and Many Times," which serve as an excellent means to acquaint pupils with the biography and work of the masters.

Encyclopaedia Britannica has a rather complete filmstrip library with such color series as "Art in Our Classroom" for primary use, and "Classroom Art for Middle Grades." These two filmstrip sets combine to demonstrate art techniques with paper and scissors, clay, stick puppets, marionettes, and crayons.

Visualizing with Art Slides

The 2 x 2″ slide has an important role in art instruction. Certain companies have available slides for art appreciation purposes. One of the leading producers of this specific type of slide is Sandak, Inc., 4 East 48th Street, New York, N.Y. 10017. The Society for Visual Education has available one-hundred 2 x 2″ color slides of traditional art masterpieces depicting great American, Dutch, German, English, French, Flemish and Italian artists, and another set of one-hundred modern art masterpieces. Another interesting set of SVE slides is entitled "Architecture Past and Present," which highlights the classical architecture of Greece and Rome.

A 2 x 2″ 35mm non-professional slide taken by the teacher, pupils and parents can be used in art lessons to point up the use of color or types of architecture in our own environment.

Motion Picture Creativity—Art Activity

The motion picture media is termed an art form and truly it is. Both the commercial and educational film producer are well aware of the use of color design in making their sets. The motion picture director must visualize, as would an artist, how a setting will look on film, and he is fully aware of how lighting can express an aesthetic quality in the setting.

Creative films like the Encyclopaedia Britannica's "Loon's Necklace" and the uniquely animated Contemporary Films' "Clay" show a blending of the talents of art and the camera technician. Imaginative film making should not be the exclusive domain of the professional and educational film producer, but schools themselves can blaze trails of creative art film. One elementary school, in the Lexington, Massachusetts area, has for years been making short motion pictures using children's art work as the basis for simplified animation. Examples of this creative art work on film have been shown on the nationwide "Today" program. Color television has given rise to a deeper application of good design, color and tonal qualities in the interior settings and scenery of such television programs.

NON-PROJECTED MATERIALS

The Element of Pictorial Reality

Graphics are classified as non-projectuals, which they are, but when they are used for art instruction purposes they are also classified as display materials. No matter how they are classified, graphics, such as pictorials taken from current magazines and newspapers, are a most important instructional device in art for they provide a focal point for art activities. They also provide an endless range of pictorials which add an essential element of reality. Even simple snapshots or photographs, especially color ones, can show picturesque landscapes or architecturally impressive buildings which could be suitable subjects for a creative art lesson.

Posters afford the teacher an opportunity to acquaint pupils with such key elements in art as color, texture, line and form. Pupil-made posters do not require expensive materials. They can be made on sundry surfaces; e.g., on wrapping paper, oaktag or construction paper. Tempera paint, crayon, felt marker and colored chalk are only a few of the materials that can be employed in posters.

As most art teachers know, a good poster should not be crammed with too many facts, lettering or objects; it should not be "busy." A lot of time should be spent at the chalkboard discussing the fundamentals of a good layout.

An Uncluttered Bulletin Board

Much of what has been said about posters can also be said about bulletin boards. The essence of a good bulletin board is that an orderly and well-balanced display becomes an appealing part of the classroom decor. Pupils should be proud to see their work put on view.

Restraint is the key word to remember in laying out a well-balanced bulletin board, one that is uncluttered, with plenty of white space showing. Of course, there are many ways to achieve an attractive bulletin board design. One technique is to place the most dominant or appealing illustration or pictorial in the top center (the optical center), with the other pieces of art visuals being placed on the board fanning out in a checkerboard pattern from the main illustration.

Unity of Bulletin Board Purpose

There is no limit to what materials can be used on bulletin boards. Some of the more popular materials are burlap, corrugated, cardboard, colored yarn or construction paper. There is no restriction to novel bulletin board ideas ranging from paper mosaics, to paper sculpture, string toys and yarn drawings. However, the themes for bulletin board displays must be of a single purpose. A good display should not be a potpourri of conflicting topics and sub-topics, but the element of unity must be apparent to the viewer.

Functional Visuals—Flannel and Chalk Boards

Flannel boards perform an important function in teaching the comparative sizes of objects. Colored felt squares and circles in assorted dimensions can be used as an object lesson or reference point for size. This visual aid may also be employed in teaching the elements of layout, so important in creating good posters and bulletin boards. The chalkboard is still considered a reliable visual for the vast majority of art teachers. The art teacher, probably more than any other teacher save possibly the math and science instructor, depends upon the chalkboard to sketch layouts and show a sequence of steps in specific art activities.

Utilizing an Art Text

Why use art textbooks? Certainly, an imaginative art teacher, who has strong training and experience, does not have to rely exclusively on textbooks. However, a new art teacher or classroom teacher with limited art background will depend on an art textbook as a guide. Certainly, the choice of the best art textbook is a must. As is the case with other subject areas, most art textbooks are well organized and contain a balanced art program. Some of the better textbooks, considered by authorities to be the most comprehensive and visually attractive for classroom instruction, are: *Our Expanding Vision* by Kelly Fearing and others, published by Benson, 1960; *My World of Art* by Blanche Jefferson, published by Allyn & Bacon, 1963; and *Growing with Art* by Maude Ellsworth and Michael Andrews, published by Singer, 1960.

ART APPRECIATION

Every school and art teacher should try to plan some sort of art appreciation program comparable to the music appreciation curriculum.

Children should learn to appreciate what makes a particular piece of art great or, furthermore, what makes great art a masterpiece. Obviously, samples of great art must be brought into the classroom or seen in field trips.

As noted earlier, the opaque projector is one means of projecting art reproductions from reference books or magazines on the screen. Another method is the use of some of the available color filmstrips that acquaint the student with certain artists and show examples of their work.

The best sources for such aids are the numerous art galleries in the country. Certainly, some of these museums should be willing to work cooperatively where inexpensive duplicates, reproductions of original masterpieces could be made accessible to schools. Many art museums make small color postcard reproductions of art work available, with the cost ranging from 10¢ to 25¢.

SCHOOL ART GALLERY

After taking your group to the local art gallery or museum, and exposing them to pure art, why not originate an art gallery of your own at your school? The school art center could take one or two forms. It could be a display of mounted reproductions cut from magazines or collections of postcards of art reproductions, or it might include some borrowed work from a local artist or art loaned from a museum.

After their exposure to a professional art form, encourage youngsters to organize their own art display with a collection of their best art endeavors, whether they are crayon, chalk, paint, papier-maché, clay or fabric. An art fair could be put on within the classroom or outdoors (Figure 10-2). It is highly recommended that, if the activity is held outdoors, the children's art work be mounted on strong cardboard to insure durability. Individual paintings and drawings can be stapled or glued to the board, attached to wire and rope, and strung across the school fence. Clothespins or large metal clasps are used to clip the art work to the rope. Masking or pressure sensitive tape could be used if the side of the school building is the only place available for display of art work.

UTILIZING THE UNIQUE

There is no limit to the imagination, and there is no restriction in the variety of materials that can be utilized in art instruction. Both the commonplace and the unusual are the raw materials for art activities; e.g., teachers may use such items as chalk, thread, yarn, pipe cleaners,

SIDEWALK ART GALLERY

by Cathy Johnson

Illustration by Cathy Johnson

Figure 10-2

Sidewalk Art Galleries

construction paper or buttons. Novel art projects can be accomplished with old newspapers, leaves, scraps of paper, cloth, feathers or pine cones.

A highly practical 88-page art book which emphasizes art projects made from a wide variety of scrap materials is "Art from Scrap," by Carl Reed and Joseph Orze, published by Davis Publications, Inc., Worcester, Mass. 01608.

Leaf Pictures One attractive art form involves the utilization of leaves from deciduous trees, evergreen needles or leaves, or perhaps even flower petals, in making unique pictures. The initial step is to outline a sketch of the figure or design desired, and then paint. Spread glue on the surface of the drawing to be touched up. Utilize fresh leaves and needles, and place them on the drawing, obtaining a most novel effect. The leaves and the drawing may be preserved by spraying them with clear shellac. Do not use dry leaves since they will easily disintegrate.

Bleach Bottle Creatures Preface this art lesson with a Dr. Seuss Story, such as "If I Ran the Zoo" or "Scrambled Eggs," with his myriad of odd

166

creatures. Have pupils re-create the wildly fantastic animals from the world of Dr. Seuss using plastic bleach containers as the basic construction material. It has been found that these plastic bottles will cut very easily if soaked in hot water. Buttons, colored construction paper, clothespins, pipe cleaners, and felt tip markers can be employed to make features.

Ten Minute Masks The simplest material to use to make masks is a paper bag. All you need do is attach buttons, colored yarn or construction paper to the paper bag, use a felt marker to complete features, cut openings for eyes and nose, and you're in business. Another variation of this is to use flat cardboard, or plastic trays in which meat and fruit are sold at the supermarket. Sketch features with a felt marker and add other features with construction paper. These extra features may be affixed with glue, paper fasteners, cord or old shoelaces; the latter also make excellent ties for the mask (Figure 10-3).

Illustration by Cathy Johnson

Figure 10-3

Ten Minute Masks

Crazy Quilt Pictures Have children bring as many odd but easily found objects as screws, tacks, torn construction paper, aluminum foil, buttons, bottle caps, straws, or colored cellophane. Later, have the group glue this wild melange on reinforced construction paper, cardboard or oaktag surface. It is recommended that the wild picture pattern be sprayed with a clear lacquer.

Disc Art   Don't lose all your buttons—use them along with rubber and metal washers or bottle caps, to make interesting figures. These items can be glued or cemented to oaktag to form imaginative outline figures; or an animal sketch may be made with a felt pen and the disc adornments added later.

SUMMARY

Art is a natural creative pursuit, and like music, it shines best in a spontaneous and informal atmosphere. Imaginative audio-visual materials enable the teacher to bring about a favorable climate for imaginative art activities. Audio-visual aids help build a firm foundation for art appreciation by bringing the past world of art into the present.

The art teacher should incorporate, to a much greater degree, projectual devices such as the opaque, overhead, filmstrip and 2 x 2″ slides in presenting lessons. Carefully selected visuals enable pupils to more clearly interpret specific art techniques and gain a deeper appreciation of art values. Projected visuals, with their tremendous power of magnification and intensity of light, bring a taste for color not usually achieved by conventional means. Art resource personnel can do much for the classroom teacher by emancipating him from conservative and drab bulletin boards in employing the basic principles of art with commonplace and new materials in a challenging manner.

11

THE ROLE OF THE
SCHOOL LIBRARIAN
IN
MULTI-MEDIA INSTRUCTION

The librarian has one of the most challenging jobs in the school. Today, the school librarian has a multiplicity of tasks, namely, the selection of books, organizing a good reference collection, preparing effective library displays and organizing bookfairs. Because of the range of her responsibilities, the role of school librarian is considered essential to the elementary school environment. Audio-visual materials such as disc recordings, overhead transparencies, filmstrips, slides, and bulletin boards can effectively assist the librarian in carrying out her instructional responsibilities.

THE AUDIO IMPETUS TO LIBRARY INSTRUCTION

The Best in Recorded Literature

The role of the elementary school librarian goes beyond basic library and reference skills. The prime library function is to increase children's *desire* to read, as well as to develop their ability to listen. In order to achieve these laudable goals, the librarian uses superb disc recordings of good children's literature and excellent readings of quality poetry for youngsters, such as those of José Ferrer and Marni Nixon. One outstanding literary appreciation series for elementary school is produced by Bowmar Records, Inc., 622 Rodier Drive, Glendale, California 91201, and entitled "The Best in Children's Literature." The sample topics in the series narrated by José Ferrer, Donald Murphy and Marni Nixon are: "Halloween Tales," "Values," "Classics for Children," "Child's World of

Sound" and "Fun with Language." A helpful feature of this series is double album jackets which contain suggestions to librarians on how to relate the story in the child's own words.

Another of the librarians' favorite record series is the twelve LP story sets produced by Weston Woods Studios, Weston, Connecticut 06880. These contain such popular stories as "Mike Mulligan and His Steam Shovel," "Chanticleer and the Fox," "The Five Chinese Brothers," "Hercules," "Make Way for Ducklings," "Curious George Rides" and "Madeline's Rescue." Another popular record album is "Ruth Sawyer Storyteller" in which the renowned storyteller narrates and comments on the art of storytelling.

Telling a Story

Records are ideal for storytelling periods and are used to interest children in good literature. There are many fine children's records on the market, but unfortunately, there are many ultra-sophisticated and overly commercialized records that tamper with the original classic and author's intent, thus making it almost unrecognizable. For instance, one recording of Washington Irving's immortal "Rip Van Winkle" is so extremely contrived and altered that, if the author were living, he would be uncontrollably enraged.

Carefully selected radio programs and tape recordings can also enhance a library period. They can motivate listening, but even more important, they can be a catalyst for pupils' comments and discussion. The National Tape Repository (Bureau of Audio-Visual Instruction of the University of Colorado, Boulder, Colorado) makes available several series of recorded stories on master tape that can be duplicated on your own tape at nominal cost. Some of the series' titles suitable for elementary school are "The World of Story," "Land of Make Believe," "Old Tales and New," "Stories in the Wind" and "Stories are for Fun."

In her concern for library skills, the librarian will find the following series of special interest: "The World at Your Fingertips" which includes "What Makes a Book?" "What's in a Word?", "Information Unlimited," "Words Across the Sea" and "Shelves of Treasure," covering such pertinent topics as encyclopedias, ideas on cataloging and the Dewey Decimal System.

Imperial International Learning, Kankakee, Illinois 60901, has made available a twenty-tape library, "Palace in the Sky" for grades 1 to 3. The favorites include "Hansel and Gretel," "Story of White Satin," "Tinder Box," "Rumpelstiltskin," and "The Fairy Shoemaker." Another imaginative series, presently being distributed by Imperial, is "Golden Anthology of Children's Verse." The series of tapes made for intermediate grade students includes such poetry selections as "The Sugar Plum Tree," "The Owl and the Pussy-Cat," "Halloween" and "Nancy Hanks."

Records and tapes on specific historical periods, such as the American Civil War and Western Expansion, could inspire reading of books with similar and related themes. Thus, the motto for the school librarian should be, "You've heard the story, now read the book!"

PROJECTED MATERIALS

Both the opaque and overhead projector are ideally suited for teaching library and reference skills. Catalog cards can be projected on a large screen, along with pages of beautifully illustrated library books. Both commercial transparencies and teacher-prepared acetates can be used in instruction on basic library skills.

Filmstrips Teach Library Skills

There are some excellent filmstrip materials which can be incorporated into a productive library period such as Weston Woods Studios' (Connecticut) expansive silent and sound filmstrip series based on famous children's stories. Eye Gate House, Inc. of Jamaica, N.Y. 11435, has a basic set of four filmstrips for the intermediate level entitled "Library Services," which explains the card catalog, Dewey Decimal System, parts of the book and the use of reference materials. The same company also distributes a more sophisticated skill series entitled "Library Research Tools" for mature upper graders. Eye Gate House has prepared a twelve-set filmstrip series entitled "Classical Literature," which includes such children's favorites as "Robinson Crusoe," "Robin Hood," "Moby Dick," "Ali Baba and the Forty Thieves," "Treasure Island" and "Ivanhoe."

Films, Television and Graphics

There are motion pictures which faithfully dramatize classic children's stories. Some of these are abridged versions made from feature Hollywood movies such as "Heidi" and "Huckleberry Finn." The larger educational movie companies, such as Coronet and Encyclopaedia Britannica, produce films which are geared strictly for school audiences. These films come equipped with manuals which give the story sequence and contain suggestions for follow-up activities.

Like the classroom teacher, the librarian can be on watch for good television programs, usually specials that dramatize children's story favorites or informal programs that deal with some phase of subject matter, such as oceanography and space exploration, currently being taught in the school.

Study prints and other graphics are an integral part of the librarian's visual repertoire. Large-sized study prints, such as those distributed by the Society of Visual Education, Chicago, Illinois, Instructional Aids, Inc., Box 293, Owatonna, Minnesota 55060 and Wards, Rochester, N.Y. 14603, can be a visual spur in stimulating interest in specific science and social studies topics.

SELECTION OF BOOKS

Librarians are always confronted with dual problems of being informed and up-to-date on the best in children's literature, and besides, setting up criteria for selection of books in the library.

One of the best ways to familiarize oneself with the vast array of children's literature is to read the authoritative guides and listings which contain guidelines for evaluating the latest books and titles for a moderate-sized collection.

The following guides are recommended: *The Elementary School Library Collection,* published by Bro-Dart Industries, Inc., 52 Earl St., Newark, New Jersey 07114; *Children's Books for Schools and Libraries,* published by R. R. Bowker Company, 1180 Avenue of the Americas, New York, N.Y. 10036; and *Best Books for Children 1969,* also published by Bowker. In addition, we have two guides which are considered to be classics on the subject: *Children's Literature in the Elementary Schools* by Charlotte S. Huck and Doris A. Young, published by Holt, Rinehart and Winston, Inc., 383 Madison Ave., New York, N.Y. 10017; and *Children and Books* by May Hill Arbuthnot, published by Scott Foresman & Co., 1900 East Lake Ave., Glenview, Ill. 60025.

There are a number of organizations that can offer information and advice in book selection and the organization of a good library: the American Association of School Librarians at 50 East Huron Street, Chicago, Illinois 60611, the U.S. Office of Education, 400 Maryland Avenue, SW, Washington, D.C. 20202 and the Children's Book Council, 175 5th Avenue, New York, N.Y. 10010.

A well-planned selection policy is a must for school librarians. The librarian can choose from a number of book selection aids before making any final decisions about what materials should be purchased. Certainly, any sound selection policy should consider the curriculum as well as opinions of the faculty. Although it is the administration and librarian that make the final decision on book purchases, the recommendations of the teaching staff should be considered at decision-making time.

Obviously, school library collections should consist of a broad sampling of fact and fiction materials. Books at the primary level must be easy for children to read, and those at the intermediate level should take into account variance in reading ability, degrees of maturity and, most important, interest level.

Knowledge of the community in which he is serving is a most important consideration for the librarian. Book selection must of necessity be guided by the economic and cultural background of the pupils in the school. Special attention in choice of books for minority groups is most important. Good literature will indicate the contribution of each culture, and treatment of fictional characters should depict minorities as respected and accepted.

There are other considerations in book selection that most materials chosen should have: namely, ethical and moral values and those which portray situations with which pupils can identify.

Books should be selected that fit the need of the slow learner, the gifted child and compulsive reader. Illustrations in books motivate pupils, stimulate their imagination, and with such factual material as science and social studies, clarify concepts.

The most important determinant of book selection is, of course, the library budget. An established library inventory should ascertain the strength and weakness of the present collection. Information on neighborhood public library collections will also be an important guideline for future purchase.

REFERENCE COLLECTION

A good reference section is the cornerstone of the school library collection. Obviously, no two schools will have the same type and size of library reference collection, just as no school has the same set of conditions as to students and academic priorities.

When we think of essential reference materials this becomes synonymous with encyclopedias, as most everyone knows encyclopedias are reference books where specific facts and statistics may be found. Most educators consider the *World Book Encyclopedia, Compton's Pictured Encyclopedia* and *Our Wonderful World* the outstanding reference works for the elementary school. For advanced readers *Collier's Encyclopedia* and *Encyclopedia International* are held in high esteem.

Two specialized reference works also highly recommended for inclusion in school libraries are: H. W. Wilson's *Junior Book of Authors* and its sequel, *More Junior Authors,* which contain a listing of biographical notes on popular authors of children's books. The American Library Association's *Subject Index to Books for Primary Grades* and *Subject Index to Books for Intermediate Grades* aid pupils to find books on specific topics. *Webster's Biographical Dictionary* gives a comprehensive list of brief descriptions of famous personalities.

Purchase of yearbooks or annuals is recommended. Not every encyclopedia has annuals; however, it is not necessary to purchase a yearbook for each encyclopedia. Yearbooks help recapitulate the past year's events, as well as to up-date the encyclopedia series with information not previously available. Almanacs are an intrinsic part of the school library reference department. The best known are the reliable *World Almanac and Book of Facts* and *Information Please Almanac.*

Specialized dictionaries, such as the new easy-to-use *New Pocket Roget's Thesaurus in Dictionary Form* and *Webster's Dictionary of Synonyms,* should also be available.

Atlases are important to the study of world geography. The most popular atlases are Goode's *Classroom Atlas* and Hammonds' *New Supreme World Atlas.*

There are many fine index reference volumes, such as Mary H. Eastman's *Index to Fairy Tales, Myths and Legends,* V. Sell's *Subject Index to Poetry for Children and Young People* and John E. Brewton's *Index to Children's Poetry.*

ROLE OF PAPERBACKS

Juvenile paperbacks are inexpensive, soft-cover replicas or reproductions of hard-cover editions of popular children's literature. Today, paperbacks are packaged attractively and, because of their size, thinness, effective printing style and light weight, do not appear as ponderous for children to read as some of the more expensive hard-cover editions. One drawback to paperbacks is that their life expectancy is not as long as their hard-covered brethren. Yet, the fact that they are so inexpensive makes them an easy-to-replace, worth-while short-term investment.

Since 1959 there has been a tremendous surge of interest in paperbacks. For the past decade most of the paperbacks have been directed toward junior high or high school audiences, but there is an increasing movement toward publishing paperbacks for elementary pupils.

Generally, paperback collections are found in the classroom, but a representative collection in the library would sustain interest in this form of printed media. Of course, there is bound to be a certain amount of resentment against the use of paperbacks in the library, for the librarian has been conditioned to using only hard-cover books. In fact, some librarians might consider the use of paperbacks in the library collection as heresy or sacrilege. An outstanding reference source for a listing of available paperbacks is *Paperbound Books in Print,* published by R. R. Bowker, 1180 Avenue of the Americas, New York, N.Y. 10036. *Scholastic Magazine,* with its popular Arrow Book Club, makes a wide variety of paperbacks available for classroom libraries at an astonishingly low cost.

LIBRARY DISPLAYS

The cardinal purpose of effective library bulletin boards is to arouse curiosity in literature and educate pupils in library reference skills. There should be no limit to the wealth of material for library displays and bulletin boards. Topics like the seasons, weather, space exploration, National Book Week, current children's literature, famous inventors, and presidents are a mere sampling of potential subject matter for an attractive bulletin board.

The important thing is that library bulletin boards should not become stagnant. An open-end bulletin board, which consists of interesting material planned by the teacher or librarian, should leave space for pupils to contribute their own ideas by means of reflective drawings, or book and research reports.

Three-dimensional effects will enhance library-oriented bulletin boards, with decorated sheets of construction paper attached to the board in such a way as to simulate real book effect. Dust jackets may be readily obtained from the book publishers, thus giving the librarian a nucleus for interesting displays. Some inventive teachers have made fascinating displays by shaping pieces of styrofoam in the various sizes of books, then encasing the styrofoam in book jackets. Construction paper silhouettes make attractive bulletin boards when contrasted with a bright background. Objects like toy cars, dolls, furniture, and items of realia such as stamps and coins, also add a realistic aura to bulletin boards. Mobiles suspended around the bulletin board add still more desirable effects. Bulletin boards can be dressed up with additional displays on easel boards, with items of realia placed on a table or with pupil-made dioramas.

Develop a challenging bulletin board built around catchy slogans. An ideal way to incur more pupil interest is to initiate a friendly competition (not monetary) where pupils are moved to prepare posters with clever captions, as, for example, for Library Week or for a bookfair.

One obvious idea for current bulletin boards is to synchronize the promotion of bulletin boards with appropriate television specials, or. to time them with recently released, outstanding children's films such as "Mary Poppins" or "Dr. Dolittle."

An outstanding bulletin board aid is the 120-page handbook, containing monthly display ideas for librarians and classroom teachers, entitled, "Library and Classroom Bulletin Boards," by Margaret Steenrod, offered by Teachers Publishing Corporation, Darien, Conn. 06820.

BOOKFAIR

One of the gala educational events of the school year for librarians is usually the bookfair. This is one time when books are certain to be popular, for children can buy books for their very own.

The underlying reason for initiating a bookfair is for the express purpose of exposing children to samples of good literature. A successful bookfair gives both pupils and their parents a chance to examine the best wares of publishers of children's books.

Bookfairs require a great deal of planning by the school librarian. A multitude of books suitable for the fair can be found in R. R. Bowker's *Best Books for Children*, American Library Association's *Subject Index to Books for Primary Grades and Intermediate Grades* and *Basic Book Collection for Elementary Grades*. Lists can also be compiled from book review sections of the *New York Times, Horn Book, School Library Journal* and *Scholastic Magazine*. A local book jobber or bookstore can also assist with selections.

For helpful techniques in the organization of a bookfair, secure a copy of *Recipe for a Book Fair*, published by Children's Book Council, 175 Fifth Avenue, N.Y. and *Seven Criteria for Book Fairs*, published by the American Library Association, 50 East Huron Street, Chicago, Illinois.

People experienced in bookfairs recommend that book lists be prepared for the year months in advance and that the eventual selections encompass several price ranges and cover a wide range of topics. Lists should include both paperbacks and hard-cover editions. Book lists should reach the supplier at least four to six months in advance so that the books may be packed, ready to be sent to you.

Courtesy of "Our Schools," Board of Education, Northport, N.Y.

Figure 11-1

Librarian Acts As Agent for Multi-Media

Librarians should also plan on having committees of adults, perhaps parents from the PTA, assist in setting up displays and unpacking, etc. Only one or two parents should handle cash and the other receipts.

The actual setting up of the display certainly should be done days in advance of the fair, either after school or preferably at night when the usual school traffic is at a minimum. Books should not be buried on tables in helter skelter fashion to simulate a bargain basement display. Pupils and parents perusing the collection should be able to examine a book without difficulty. Provisions for petty cash receipts, simplified order forms, booking procedures and bags for the books sold, are just a few of the important details which must be attended to if the bookfair is to run smoothly. Books on sale at bookfairs are usually sold on the spot from the inventory on hand, or books may be ordered and paid for in advance and shipped by the distributor upon receipt of the order. Several workers should gather the unsold books and prepare them for shipping to jobbers or bookstores. The remaining workers could assist in checking receipts and money against the lists of books sold.

SUMMARY

The role of school librarian is becoming increasingly more important with the passage of time. The school librarian's tasks are becoming more complex. He is responsible for teaching pupils library and reference skills, providing extensive enrichment and research facilities, and finding the best avenue in which to foster student interest in reading. Recently, the school library has become the audio-visual aids distribution center; thus, librarians are not only being entrusted with book services, but acting as agents for multi-media instruction (Figure 11-1).

12

COORDINATING PHYSICAL EDUCATION THROUGH AUDIO-VISUAL TECHNIQUES

At this time it must be truthfully said that, while there are audio-visual materials available for physical education instruction, there is obviously a need for further research in ways in which these tools can be utilized to a greater extent.

The best audio device for covering a diverse range of physical education activities is the phonograph. It is probably the most dependable aural aid in instructing pupils in physical fitness, learning poise and in the mastery of dancing techniques.

The overhead projector and 8mm film loops are perhaps the most promising of the newer visual media. The overhead is perfect for large group gym instruction, while the 8mm film loop is an attractive device best suited for individualized and informal instruction. As time passes, more techniques and activities will be developed in connection with the utilization of these newer projectual media.

Display materials such as the bulletin board, flannel board and chalkboard are the basic vehicles for motivating greater interest in gym activities and sports events. As with any subject, it always pays to advertise.

NONVERBAL EXPERIENCES

Be Wise—Exercise!

In recent years there has been a decided improvement in the physical fitness of students now attending our nation's elementary school. However, all experts on physical education agree that there is room for even further improvement, and perhaps audio-visual materials can do their part in helping pupils develop greater athletic skills, learn teamwork and learn how to keep bodies in top physical condition.

Mastering Basic Locomotive Skills

In the lower grades the physical education program is built around nonverbal experiences, with stress on physical fitness and learning basic locomotion skills. Primary age children must become involved in simple motion activities like marching, skipping, hopping or running. It is important at this age level for children to learn how to climb, crawl and swing on both gym and playground equipment. Simple acrobatics—for example, forward and backward rolls—should be taught. Pupils should also become actively engaged in rhythm and imitative activities, even if just a bean bag toss.

When we reach the intermediate level in school, there is no lessening of effort in the goal of achieving greater physical fitness and manual dexterity. During these years there is an increasing emphasis on calisthenics. Many schools also give attention to those who have exceptional gymnastic abilities, as well as those who need special attention because of poor motor reflexes.

Learning the Fundamentals

Boys and girls in the upper grades are instructed in the fundamentals of individual, dual or team sports. It is most important, as pupils master the basics of any sport, that they also learn the tenets of good sportsmanship. The gym curriculum is also concerned with an extension of learning more advanced stunts such as headstands, cartwheels and tumbling.

The following resource material is recommended: The American Association for Health, Education and Recreation has several publications that are helpful to novice or experienced gym teachers, such as *How We Do It Game Book, Classroom Activities, Outdoor Education, Rhythmic Activities* and *After-School Games and Sports;* and the N.E.A., Dept. of Rural Education's *Physical Education in Small Schools.*

AUDIO MATERIALS

Records: the Audio Gym Aid

There are many fine series of records available for gym activities: Educational Activities Inc., 1937 Grand Ave., Baldwin, N.Y. 11510, has a four-record set called "Fitness Fun for Everyone," a suitable 78 rpm for grades K-3, a two-record $33\frac{1}{3}$ set for elementary and junior high grades titled "And the Beat Goes on for Physical Education" with an accompanying illustrated manual. Other record sets, all 78 rpm, are "Postural Improvement Activities" and "Modern Dynamic Physical Fitness Activities."

A brand new three-record series, "Developmental Exercises Music and Calls," produced by Hoctor Educational Records, Waldwick, N.J., teaches physical education in the manner advocated by the President's Council on Physical Fitness. The first record is made for grades one and two. The second is intended for grades three and four, and the final record in the set is geared for grades five and six. An interesting feature of this set is that the centerfold of each record jacket contains teaching hints and helpful photos. Another distinguishing characteristic is that the series employs European and American folk music for melodic backdrop.

Hop, Skip and Jump

The Sing 'n Do Company, Inc. of Midland Park, New Jersey, has recently made available a six-record, $33\frac{1}{3}$ album of musical stories, suitable for physical fitness fun and classroom relaxation periods for grades kindergarten, one and two. The premise of these records is to involve children in such activities as prancing, running, turning, knee bending and marching within the framework of musical creative stories. Each record has engagingly employed an appealing special events or holiday theme for a diversified set of exercises; e.g., "Fireman Joe, a Fire Prevention Program," involves chopping, steering and pumping; "The Ringmaster," a circus-oriented theme, calls for children to perform such individualized exercises as trotting, sidestepping and bowing; "Paper Doll" highlights Christmas and Easter themes stimulating children to stand, sit, slide and touch their toes and sway without letting go of their hands (Figure 12-1).

Com'on Let's Dance!

RCA Company Record Division, 155 E. 34 Street, New York, N.Y. is distributing a freshly imaginative, LP $33\frac{1}{3}$, eight-record series that effectively combines music and pictures in a magical amalgam for exercises, pantomime, beginning dance techniques and creative rhythms. Each album is accompanied by a 32- to 48-page storybook in full color. Some of the spritely titles are: "The Brave Hunter," "The Toy Tree," and "Flappy and Floppy" (Figure 12-2 and Figure 12-3).

Illustration by Cathy Johnson

Figure 12-1
Hop, Skip and Jump Activities

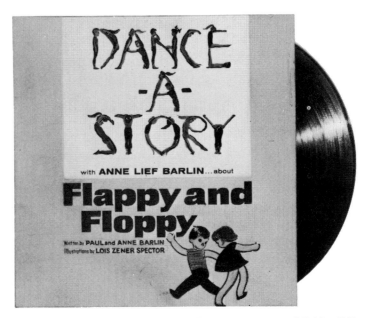

Figure 12-2

Dance a Story

Toy Tree from RCA's "Dance a Story"

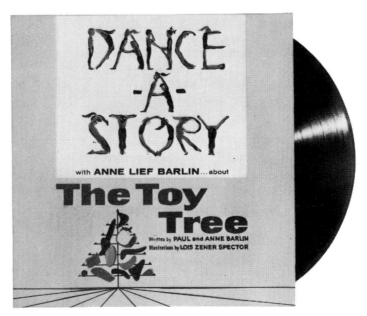

Figure 12-3

Flappy and Floppy

Another creative record album in the "Dance-a-Story" series.

PROJECTED MATERIALS

Action-Packed Visuals

The opaque in physical education can be used primarily to heighten interest in athletics. Snapshots taken at sports events, and magazine and newspaper illustrations showing sporting happenings, may be projected on the large screen. A great deal can be learned from sports-in-action pictures, which can lead to profitable classroom discussion and eventually to a better understanding of the fundamentals of a sport.

Overhead transparencies can be used in coaching sports. They are particularly useful in explaining plays, the techniques of positions and to clarify the complexities of team sports. With the help of this visual aid, team strategy for the big game can be mapped out with a minimum of effort.

The Society for Visual Education, Chicago, Illinois, has an extremely expansive filmstrip library on practically all phases of physical education. There are color sets on physical fitness and sets on team sports like baseball, basketball, badminton, tumbling, archery and wrestling gymnastics. There are other interesting titles on lifesaving and competitive swimming. Most of these filmstrips have complementary teacher and student manuals, imaginatively written, and many sound versions which have explanatory narration recorded on $33\frac{1}{3}$ rpm records. The Stanley Bowmar Company, Inc., 4 Broadway, Valhalla, N.Y. 10595, distributes a two-color filmstrip set, with LP records and teaching manuals, with the following titles: "Why Physical Education?" and "Citizenship Training Through Physical Education," intended for intermediate age audiences.

Slides can be used to stimulate interest in sport activities. Pictures taken by teacher, pupil and parents at a sporting event can be shown for all to enjoy. Slides could also be taken which illustrate fundamentals or steps in specific sports activities.

8mm Film Loop Revolution

Most schools will not find it a problem to secure many of the professionally-sponsored films, especially on baseball. Most major league clubs make their promotional films available to educators at no cost. Some of these are purely educational films that demonstrate skills in sports and cover the fundamentals. Perhaps the biggest boon to the gym teacher is the introduction of 8mm single concept film loops which allow the viewer to see specialized sports techniques close up, and probably more effectively than the conventional 16mm trade films. Some enterprising gym teachers have taken their own 8mm films, which can be put in cartridges supplied by Technicolor, Inc., 1300 Frawley Dr., Costa Mesa, Calif. 92627, for a nominal fee (Figure 12-4 and Figure 12-5).

Courtesy of Technicolor Corporation, Costa Mesa, California

Figure 12-4

Technicolor Film Loop Projector

One type of 8mm film loop projector.

Courtesy of Fairchild Camera & Instrument Corp., Plainview, N.Y.

Figure 12-5

Fairchild 8mm Film Loop Sound Projector

Fairchild's Mark IV with "MoviePak" employs the new sound film cartridge—allows user to change films in a matter of seconds.

The Society for Visual Education, Chicago, Illinois, is the leading producer of skill builders and has a very extensive inventory of 8mm and Super 8mm film loops which permit students to carefully examine and analyze the performance of gymnastic experts. The titles include "Tumbling," "Side Horse," "Vaulting," "Floor Exercises," and "Parallel Bars." Another film loop producer, Film Associates, Los Angeles, California, distributes 8mm and Super 8mm cartridge series on techniques involved in such team sports as basketball and volleyball, as well as individual activities such as weight training.

Wide World of Sports

A lot can be learned from television practically every week, especially on weekends when some major sporting event like baseball and golf is being telecast. Many local stations show sports films on golf, bowling and other sports, which show many useful techniques for the novice.

NON-PROJECTED MATERIALS

Physical education can be easily correlated to other such curriculum areas as music and art; e.g., charts on physical achievement or posters advertising gym activities like intramurals. If a dance program is being put on under the auspices of the physical education department, students could work on invitations.

This Way for the Gym Display

Some imaginative physical education teachers have set up bulletin board displays which highlight school activities, perhaps calisthenics or gymnastics. All pupils are asked to do is to make drawings depicting various exercises. A committee of students could make a large-scale mural showing a composite of various sports activities.

The flannel board and chalkboard, utilized in much the same manner as the overhead transparency, can be an effective vehicle for physical education, serving as a visual coaching device, thus enabling pupils to understand plays in football and basketball.

AUDIO-VISUAL INSPIRED ACTIVITIES

Medieval Tournament Shades of King Arthur and Ivanhoe! Why not correlate the social studies curriculum with physical education? An ideal activity is to put on a tournament modeled after the ones that took place in Europe during the Middle Ages. A typical activity is one in which boys engage in a rope-climbing contest of skill, where they are only allowed the use of their hands, in a simulated exercise much like the knights storming the castle to rescue the fair lady. Another suggested activity is one in which a bamboo pole is hurled by contestants at a mock target pasted to the gym wall, simulating a lance-throwing test of knightly skill. All these imaginative exercises in physical skill could inspire research in social studies.

Physical Fitness Scrapbook   In keeping with the objectives of the President's Physical Fitness Program, encourage pupils to make a scrapbook that consists of photographs or magazine illustrations that show various physical activities being performed.

Stick Figure Gymnastics   With the art teacher's assistance, have pupils utilize black construction paper, colored straws, pipe cleaners and scraps of materials to make little stick figures showing good posture and doing simple exercises. Circular pieces of colored cloth could represent the head, straw or pipe cleaners the limbs. If this is too difficult, have pupils make a series of posters with a felt pen showing stick figures in various positions or postures.

Let's Dance!   Dancing has long been a favorable form of exercise. Why not set up committees to practice various types of ballroom dancing or folk dancing? When sufficiently polished, invite others to see the dance. Dances of foreign countries could also be the subject of a combined gym-music program. If you really want to add a colorful touch, dress pupils in appropriate but simple costumes.

The History of Sports   A most fascinating activity, which could be correlated with the language arts or library program, would involve researching the origin and the history of individual or team sports. Pupil research reports on the various sports could be placed on the bulletin board adjacent to the gymnasium or some other prominent display corner.

Follow My Direction   The tape recorder can be put to good use when the teacher records the commands for activities such as calisthenics and permits the pupil to make on-the-spot observations of the group. For primary students, why not put an old exercise favorite, "Simon Says" on tape?

SUMMARY

Physical education should not be a "just for fun" period. It should be integrated and coordinated with other subject areas such as language arts, social studies, music and art. Certainly, audio-visual aids can help facilitate the correlation of subject matter areas to the activities of the gym class. Yes, audio-visual aids can be an integral part of the President's Physical Fitness Program!

13

AUDIO-VISUAL PREPARATIONS
FOR FIELD TRIPS
AND USE OF
COMMUNITY RESOURCES

To many pupils and almost all teachers a field trip is usually one of the major events of the school year. It enables the pupils to break away from the confines of the classroom and permits them to use the community as a laboratory for learning. Because of the direct involvement of pupils, field trips are categorized as personalized learning experiences. One thing is certain, however: no other audio-visual activity requires as much preparation as the field trip. Yet, there cannot be anything with as much educational impact on the pupil as this self-same field trip.

"There's gold in this here community," is a phrase we teachers should use more often. If we explore what is available in our own communities, we may be amazed at the wealth of resources available to us.

ASCERTAINING PUPILS' NEEDS FOR A FIELD TRIP

Is this field trip necessary? A school journey that is poorly planned, and without any educational purpose and meaningful activity, is a sheer waste of everyone's time. A field trip should have true significance for students. It should enhance the curriculum and provide personalized experiences that would be hard to find in the ordinary classroom environment.

Any visitation must take into account pupil interests, desires and necessities. The best way to evaluate pupil needs is to listen casually to their conversations and look for an indication of specific interests, in their written work or oral reports. The subject area, age and maturity of pupils should help the teacher determine the eventual site for a field trip.

TYPES OF TRIPS

Field trips can be made to neighboring communities, or be a pilgrimage to places beyond the school's limits. They can be of short duration, of either a class period or a full day, or of longer duration, two to three days, or even a week. The trip may be based on science, social studies, math or language arts topics. Most trips are primarily informational in nature, generally undertaken to motivate learning, for review work and to supplement or enrich the particular subject area being studied in class.

OBJECTIVES

The school journey must have clearly defined objectives if it is to be a successful learning experience. First, the location of the facility to be visited ought to be investigated, and once the selection is made, should be one that will excite students. The successful trip should accelerate interest in learning and bridge a knowledge gap that could not otherwise be filled in by strictly textual and audio-visual materials. A field trip provides pupils with a vicarious experience, and the activities connected with the visitation should assist students to recall associated skills therewith, and to add to previous learning experiences, thus building their apperceptive background.

EVALUATING COMMUNITY RESOURCES

When looking for suitable places for the class to visit, why not evaluate what is available in one's own and a neighboring community before planning longer, and perhaps more extensive and expensive trips? Actually, for primary age children, trips of short duration are probably more fitting and less tiring.

There are several ways to compile a list of potential local sites to visit. One means is to contact the local Chamber of Commerce or some other responsible civic group. Fellow teachers, parents and even pupils can indeed provide the average teacher with sufficient leads. It is important, after selecting a site for visitation, to find out if the particular organization or facility wishes to be visited.

GUIDELINES AND PROCEDURES FOR ORGANIZING SCHOOL JOURNEYS

There are a number of necessary steps and procedures that are pre-requisites for any school journey. It is imperative that field trips be well-organized, since there is usually a large number of children involved. First, no trip can be planned without the authorization or blessing of the school. The teacher, before asking the administration, must be clear on the objectives of the trip and be prepared to state to what extent such a trip will enhance a pupil's learning experience. The teacher must also possess facts about the length of the trip, what is to be seen, transportation requirements and estimated costs.

An alert instructor, after ascertaining the expenses involved in the trip, must plan a sound way to raise money for the trip. In many schools, most children have the money for the trip, but there are always pupils who may not have the financial resources to go. Every school and teacher should have some plan to take care of these youngsters without it having the stigma of "charity." If permitted, fund-raising activities, such as class cake sales or class dues or proceeds from pupil entertainments, can be used. Sometimes the PTA and community groups or the school itself will make funds available for these underprivileged youngsters.

PRE-PLANNING AND PREPARATION OF PUPILS FOR A PROJECTED TRIP

It goes without saying that all trips off the school grounds must be properly chaperoned, and written parental permission obtained. The teacher should also investigate liability and safety regulations for field trips in his school district. Liability and safety rules vary from state to state and in different school systems. Buses should be chartered from reputable carriers that have good equipment and are insured.

Most parents, if they have sufficient information about the trip, are assured that it is being supervised and know what precautions will be observed, will give their permission. Obviously, factors of supervision and safety of a proposed trip are paramount to the thoughts of most parents, and rightly so.

A word should be said about scheduling field trips: Naturally, school trips should never be scheduled during test periods or close to a holiday.

Special teachers and the cafeteria should be advised well in advance of the trip so that they can adjust their own schedule. Since inclement weather or transportation problems can cause cancellation of a trip, alternate dates should be considered in the permission slips sent home for parents' signatures.

There are other pertinent details that must be observed. For example, if a long trip is planned, lunch and rest room facilities should be checked out well in advance. One item which is a must is that several first aid kits should be obtained. It is also wise to invite two responsible parents and other adults to assist you with supervision on the trip.

There are two other phases of pupil preparation prior to a field trip. One is concerned with the actual mechanics of the trip, such as collecting the permission slips and money and possibly assigning pupils to bus seats. There should be a thorough discussion of how pupils should behave on the trip and what they should do if they somehow get separated from the group or are taken ill. There also should be discussion of how pupils should dress and what personal items they may bring along with them.

The second phase of the trip involves orientation of what the pupil is expected to see or learn on the trip. It is a prerequisite that the teacher has thoroughly read literature on the subject matter of the field study. An alert teacher will make up a list of things that the children can expect to see on their visitation. Some teachers make mimeographed or dittoed copies of the final itinerary to be distributed to pupils. Pupils should also be given the opportunity to become familiar with the subject by doing extensive reading of library reference books. If available, filmstrips and motion pictures concerned with the topic under study could round out the orientation.

CONDUCT OF THE TRIP

The more thought given to planning and preparation for a field trip, the smoother things should progress on the actual trip. Before the trip and from time to time during the trip, a head count must be taken. The teacher should remain in the background during the trip, but be constantly alert to give any directions or information required. The teacher's role is basically guide and leader, and not a disinterested sightseer. Teachers should not dominate the field trip with personal opinion or try to influence pupils in any way. Children should be permitted to make their own observations (Figure 13-1 and 13-2).

Courtesy P.S. 257, Brooklyn—Ralph T. Brande, Principal

Figure 13-1

Conduct on Field Trip—Bus

Courtesy P.S. 257, Brooklyn—Ralph T. Brande, Principal

Figure 13-2

Conduct on Field Trip—Florist

FIELD TRIP ACTIVITIES

Depending on the length of the trip and the type of transportation, it is wise to plan imaginative and quiet activities that will occupy pupils' thoughts. Pupils can get very restless on a long bus journey. One good idea is to make dittoed puzzles and riddle sheets. Some teachers make up a list of landmarks that they will pass by on the bus and suggest that pupils check off all the items they observe. Children might also be encouraged to take along a small memo book, inexpensive diary or portable tape recorder to help keep a record or to give an aural account of the trip.

Inexpensive paperbacks might be taken along. Expensive library books might be lost in the haste of embarking and disembarking on the trip. One problem with reading on a bus or train is the constant jarring. Oral games patterned after television's "What's My Line?" or old-fashioned spelling bees, are suitable activities on this educational excursion. Some teachers encourage singing on a trip, which is perfectly all right if it does not bother or distract the driver and adults accompanying the class on the journey.

FOLLOW-UP ACTIVITIES AFTER THE VISITATION

During the field trip, pupils who may have taken pictures with their cameras, should be encouraged to bring in the pictorial results for all to share. Some pupils might find the field trip to be a good starting point for making a field trip scrapbook which could contain drawings of things they have seen. Class discussion can correct any misconceptions formed during the trip. The desire for further clarification will logically lead to research reports, construction of dioramas, original stories or dramatic plays.

EVALUATION OF FIELD TRIPS

The final phase of the field trip should be concerned with our original question, "Was this field trip necessary?" This leads to a review and evaluation of the visitation by both pupils and teacher. Generally, a well-organized field trip is worth all the effort. The best measure of effectiveness is what takes place after the trip, such as a pupil's enthusiasm, the nature of class discussions and the quality of written work.

COMMUNITY RESOURCE FILE

Perhaps one of the most important things a classroom teacher or even an entire school can do is to organize a community resource file. A community resource file is a place where written information about important places, names and addresses of key personalities visited are listed either in indexed file folders, or written or typed on 5 x 8″ index cards. It is heartily recommended that information recorded in the folders and index cards be arranged in alphabetical order or cataloged according to units of work. The file folder or card should contain all pertinent information, such as the name of a person or organization to contact, the address, phone number and a résumé of what can be seen at the facility. Resource personalities who are willing to lecture or offer presentations at school should also be included in the resource file, with a short annotation of what the person has to share with the pupils.

HOW TO UTILIZE LOCAL RESOURCES

Most community resources are logical subjects for future field trip visitations, but often we can bring these community resources directly into the class. In every community there are many adults who have interesting jobs or fascinating hobbies or who possess unusual skills. Children will appreciate having the opportunity to listen to and query these visitors. It is commendable to have the resource personality come directly into class, but sometimes the same end result might be accomplished through a tape recorded interview, loan of exhibits, motion pictures and literature—the important point is to use these resource people.

SUMMARY

The success of a field trip most often will depend upon the extent of the teacher's planning and how carefully and thoughtfully he has oriented his class before the visitation. There are a myriad of details and much responsibility for the teacher in initiating any field trip. Despite all the time and effort and frustration involved, a good field trip is worth all the energy because no other medium can give so much gratification and learning enjoyment. Here is a set of guidelines for the classroom teacher for a field trip:

Pre-Planning Stage

I. Ascertaining the merits of a field trip.

    a. Determine the need for a field trip and the kind of visitation most appropriate for students of your grade level.

    b. Find out from informal discussion with the class the type of trip about which they would be most enthusiastic.

    c. Correlate the field trip as much as possible with specific subject areas; i.e., social studies, mathematics, etc.

II. Discuss the proposed trip with superiors, noting:

    1. Length of trip and itinerary.

    2. Transportation arrangements.

    3. Expenses of trip.

    4. Secure parental permission slips and discuss utilization of adult chaperones.

    5. Have available information on facilities of site to be visited, especially about lunchroom and restroom facilities.

    6. Select an appropriate date on the school calendar and alternate dates for trip in case of any last-minute cancellation.

III. Information for parents

    a. Prepare a notice about the field trip for parents supplying all pertinent information including the purpose of the trip, location of site, date of trip, supervisory arrangements, lunch arrangements, etc.

    b. Contact class mothers or other responsible adults to assist in supervision on the trip.

IV. Orientation of Pupils

    a. Full discussion of purpose of the trip.

    b. Discuss ground rules of deportment expected and advise pupils what to do in an emergency.

    c. Provide meaningful activities related to the theme of field trip prior to the visitation.

    d. Send home permission slips.

    e. Consideration of seating arrangements on bus or train.

The Day of the Trip

1. Secure First Aid kit from nurse before leaving school.
2. Take attendance.
3. If parents are assisting in supervision, give each adult a list of students to assist you in supervising the group.
4. Give pupils a checklist of items or points or interest they may observe while traveling on the trip or at the site to be visited.
5. Prepare a dittoed or mimeographed list containing a series of seat activities, such as riddles, quiet games, songs, especially for long field trips.

Field Trip Follow-Up Activities

1. Have a class discussion about the trip as soon as possible after the trip.
2. Have pupils show snapshots they may have taken of the trip or display any souvenirs such as postcards or specimens they may have bought while on the visitation.
3. Utilize any audio-visual materials that could serve as a review of trip objectives as well as to supplement knowledge gained on the trip.
4. Have the class write individual thank you letters to the authorities at the installations visited.
5. Have pupils write compositions, give oral or written reports, make drawings, or participate in research activities related to the field trip.

14

EFFECTIVE UTILIZATION
OF FREE
AND INEXPENSIVE
AUDIO-VISUAL MATERIALS

Being free or inexpensive doesn't mean that a brochure is worthwhile. In some instances this statement is true, but on the whole, a substantial percentage of the material distributed by government organizations and businesses is valuable, and most educators would agree that the advantages of free and inexpensive items far outweigh their shortcomings. Most organizations, in order to create good public relations, attempt to make their material worthy and effective for classroom use.

ADVANTAGES

What never ceases to amaze most teachers is the enthusiastic reception that these gratis materials receive from children. Even youngsters who have a great many toys and books at home are interested in these materials. Perhaps this is due to the fact that possession of these free items gives pupils a sense of ownership.

Since most printed free materials come in pamphlet or booklet form, they can be published and distributed in a relatively short time. This feature makes available more up-to-date material to the ultimate consumer. A great variety of materials ranging from charts to booklets, sample kits and free filmstrips, covers a range of subject matter and is an ideal supplement to units in science, health, social studies and math. From the teacher's viewpoint, free and inexpensive materials are ideal fodder for attractive bulletin board displays.

OBJECTIONS

As with any educational material, there are certain disadvantages with such media, and an alert teacher will sort out the good from the bad. Since some companies do distribute materials free and do have an investment, the teacher must constantly be on guard against misrepresentation and material that obviously represents only one viewpoint on a subject. The teacher must attempt to analyze the company's motives for making this matter available. Did the company publish its material as a public service, in order to nurture a better public relations image, or did they have some ulterior motive? No one will object to a limited amount of advertising as long as it does not run out of bounds. In the final analysis, most decisions on suitability of the material must rest with the classroom teacher, librarian and the school administrator.

LOCATING FREE MATERIALS

The best way to locate free materials is to go to the numerous resource guides and magazine columns where these materials are reviewed and evaluated. A list of source guides will be found at the end of this chapter. For evaluation of current materials, see magazines such as *Grade Teacher, The Instructor, Educational Screen AV Guide, Audiovisual Instructor* and *Today's Education.*

After locating sources of free material, the teacher should send for the items in a well-written letter on school stationery. In the letter, the teacher must clearly enumerate the items desired, stating the quantity needed and the purpose for which they will be used. It is also advisable to mention the grade you are teaching and the age group. It is plain old-fashioned courtesy and good public relations to thank the sponsor for making the materials available. A few compliments go a long way in encouraging sponsors to continue making these items obtainable.

CATALOGING FREE MATERIALS

Sometimes teachers fear that their mailbox will explode with free material mail. The samples of free materials themselves can be sorted and filed for future use. A good idea is to make up a special file on either 3 x 5″, 4 x 6″, or 5 x 8″ cards which, under topic headings, will enumerate pertinent items such as the title of the object, a short description of its contents, the name and address of the sponsor, and a short paragraph about the suitability and utilization. The only problem with such a file is that, without a periodic culling of the index, it will very quickly become outdated.

GUIDEBOOKS FOR SOURCES OF FREE MATERIALS

Catalog of Free Teaching Materials, Gordon Salisbury, P.O. Box 1075, Ventura, California 95002.

Educators Guide to Free Films, Educators Progress Service, Randolph, Wisconsin 53404.

Educators Guide to Free Filmstrips, Educators Progress Service, Randolph, Wisconsin 53404.

Educators Guide to Free Social Studies Material, Educators Progress Service, Randolph, Wisconsin 53404.

Educators Guide to Free Tapes, Scripts and Transcriptions, Educators Progress Service, Randolph, Wisconsin 53404.

Educators Index to Free Materials, Educators Progress Service, Randolph, Wisconsin 53404.

Sources of Free and Inexpensive Educational Materials, Esther Dever, P.O. Box 186, Grafton, West Virginia 26354.

Sources of Free and Inexpensive Materials, Educational Division, Field Enterprises, Educational Corp., Merchandise Mart Plaza, Chicago, Illinois 60654.

Sources of Free and Inexpensive Teaching Aids, Bruce Miller, Box 369, Riverside, California 92502.

Sources of Free Pictures, Bruce Miller, Box 369, Riverside, California 92502.

Sources of Free Travel Posters, Bruce Miller, Box 369, Riverside, California 92502.

Where to Get and How to Use Free and Inexpensive Teaching Aids, Robert L. Schain and Murray Pelner, Teachers Practical Press, Inc., Englewood Cliffs, New Jersey 07632.

15

AUDIO-VISUAL TRENDS, INNOVATIONS, AND TEACHING CONCEPTS IN THE CHANGING CURRICULUM

A sense of electric excitement is in the air concerning the changes taking place in the educational community today and what it portends for tomorrow. Certainly, the techniques of the schools of the future are going to be a far cry from the conservative practices over the past one-hundred fifty years of American history. More and more, words like team teaching, individualized instruction, Dial Access, programmed learning, listening carrels, non-graded school and computer-assisted education are becoming as familiar as the self-contained classroom, the textbook and chalkboard.

It is obvious that teachers will not only have to be masters of subject matter, but also they will be thoroughly familiar with the latest educational methods. And they must possess some insight into the innovative technology that will be an integral part of the new educational revolution. Audio-visual aids will certainly play an important role in this new educational climate in the promising and challenging world of tomorrow.

In tomorrow's schools, class size will fluctuate depending on the nature of the learning activity. There will be times when large group instruction is desirable, such as for films, assemblies, debates or television. Small class size is prescribed for such activities as committee work, independent study and discussion seminars.

Flexibility will not be merely a word, but a basic principle or guideline for tomorrow's teacher. For years we have been hearing about the ideal class size being set between 25 and 30. Actually, this arbitrary size is never effective for either large or small group instruction.

AUDIO-VISUAL PROGRAMS FOR THE WORLD OF TOMORROW

The world of audio-visual aids is an ever changing world. We marvel at the number of attractive audio-visual materials such as the tape recorder, slide, filmstrip projector, television and overhead projector, but these materials as equipment rest only on the first plateau of audio-visual technology. Such innovations as programmed instruction, Dial Access, language laboratory and computer-assisted instruction will enable both pupils and teacher to scale academic heights never before attainable.

ESEA Title III

Both the government and private industry have encouraged innovation and experimentation in education. The government's role in stimulating innovations has been primarily under Title III of the Elementary and Secondary School Act of 1965. This act was passed by Congress for the express purpose of encouraging creative ideas and aiding in the development of innovative elementary and secondary instructional patterns to serve as a blueprint for their establishment in a regular school program. ESEA funds have been made available to the educational community for worthy and truly innovative educational projects in any geographic region in the United States.

In order to make application for the Title III grant, it is recommended that you first secure ESEA Title III guidelines from your department of education in coordination with the Division of Plans and Supplies, U.S. Office of Education, Washington, D.C.

A recently published handbook by the Macmillan Company School Department, New York, N.Y. 10022, entitled *Federal Aid for Schools (1967-1968 Guide)* contains step by step instructions on how to define, select, write and submit proposals for educational grant programs under the National Defense Education Act.

Project Discovery

One of the most recent non-government, innovative educational projects has been the Project Discovery Program of the Bell & Howell and

Encyclopaedia Britannica companies. Under this program, specially selected schools in Shaker Heights, Ohio, Washington, D.C., Terrell, Texas
and Daly City, California receive extensive film and filmstrip libraries as
well as 16mm motion picture and 35mm filmstrip projectors for the
purpose of studying the effectiveness of these materials in improving classroom instruction (Figure 15-1).

Courtesy of Encyclopaedia Britannica, Educational Corp., Chicago, Ill.

Figure 15-1

"Project Discovery"—Shaker Heights, Ohio

Children in school in Shaker Heights, Ohio, are able to cover more subject matter by
means of motion pictures under "Project Discovery" program.

Programmed Learning

Perhaps the most challenging instructional innovation is programmed learning. Programmed learning can best be termed a self-instructional technique under which the pupil can advance in the study of a particular subject at his individual pace. When this technique was first introduced, it was in association with teaching machines. Now there is less utilization of these machines. Yet, most of the principles elicited by programmed instruction have become an integral part of computer-assisted instruction and may be adapted to printed texts.

In programmed instruction, the subject content area is broken down into a series of small steps; each step contains a series of questions and statements in the present sequence which are designed to elicit a response from the learner. In one way, we might say the program itself actually serves in the role of tutor for a student. The program can be presented in several forms. It may be encased in what is termed a teaching machine or housed in programmed textbooks. The questions are usually formulated so that the learner has a choice of completing a blank, selecting one of the multiple choice answers, or indicating agreement or disagreement by designating a positive or negative reply. One advantage of this visual aid is that it allows for self-correction as it permits the pupil to check his response; and if it is correct, the student may proceed with the lesson.

Even the strongest advocates of programmed learning materials do not recommend that this medium be used as an end in itself or act as a replacement for the classroom teacher. In fact, the strongest argument for these materials is that they free the teacher from tedious drill so that he may devote additional time to developing creative and motivational activities. Other audio-visual aids should be used in concert with programmed learning materials for a truly well-balanced and stimulating instructional program.

Dial Access—a Multi-Media Learning Center

The amazing Dial Access Retrieval System is an audio-visual innovation which incorporates learning center carrels with recorded tapes and headphones to offer the very best in creative instruction. Such a center may encompass the multi-media approach giving individual pupils quick and random access to a choice of motion picture films, audio tape, pre-programmed tapes and closed circuit television with literally just a flick of a dial by the pupil at his learning station.

Foreign Language in Our Schools

Experiences of the Armed Forces during World War II brought out an awareness of the fact that the traditional language teaching of the past decades was truly a failure. Most foreign language instruction prior to World War II involved learning strictly printed matter, with an obsession for grammar analysis and mastery of vocabulary, rather than one concentrating on fluency. The National Defense Education Act of 1958 is considered to be a turning-point in foreign language instruction, as it declared audio-oral language teaching of national interest, and since then it has made available millions of federal dollars to improve foreign language teaching.

A successful foreign language program at the elementary level is dependent upon a well versed language specialist who makes extensive use of appropriate audio-visual materials such as the overhead and tape recorder. Educational television programs and motion pictures based on foreign language are ideal substitutes for a live performance, since these media employ an expert and experienced teacher who knows native pronunciation and has an authentic language background on which to draw.

The foreign language laboratory of tomorrow will probably be the main instructional force in teaching language. This laboratory will provide an environment where pupils utilize listening carrels where they will be taught by means of audio tapes and disc recordings enhanced by such sophisticated audio-visuals as the 8mm film loop sound projector.

Computer-Assisted Instruction

Computer-assisted instruction is a comparative newcomer to the world of audio-visual aids, but it is a medium with tremendous potential, and it most certainly will have a dominant influence on education for generations to come. In recent years, industry, government and the commercial communications fields have been successfully employing computers with which to run their operations more effectively. However, in the field of education, much more groundwork and experimentation must be done before it becomes an integral fixture in the school community. Certainly, if this promising teaching system is destined to be adopted on a nationwide basis, numerous problems in financing the necessary installations and securing programming information must be overcome.

The basic value of employing computers in the learning process is the ability to store and dispense knowledge, and the capacity to individualize instruction with a higher degree of efficiency than can be achieved by the conventional teaching methods of the past.

Computer-assisted instruction, or CAI, was initially developed by many of the people responsible for the evolution of programmed learning materials, and much of what has been proven successful in programmed learning has been adapted and modified for computer-assisted instruction. Actually, programmed learning materials are only one aspect of this awe-inspiring medium.

A pupil can sit at a console (Figure 15-2) where a typewriter is used, activated by telephone lines, permitting the pupil and computer to exchange information. A distinctive feature of computer-assisted instruc-

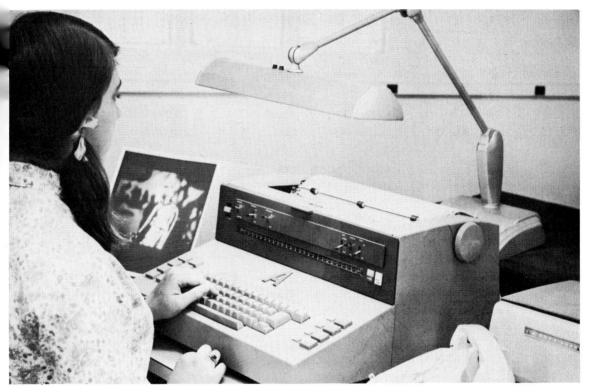

Credit to Board of Cooperative Educational Services, Yorktown Heights, N.Y.

Figure 15-2

Computer-Assisted Instruction (CAI)

In this CAI situation the pupil is seated at a typewriter terminal which types out descriptions of problems and instructions prompted by slides and tape recordings. A student responds by typing in her answer which in turn is analyzed and reacted to by the computer.

tion is that it effectively employs the newer and more promising multi-media systems. For example, this electronic wizard utilizes 8mm and 16mm film loops and video tape recorder, television, slides and filmstrips to drill and tutor students, and promote a spirit of inquiry within the pupil himself. Will CAI evoke major changes in the role of the teacher and affect school environment? The answer, a resounding "yes," may be looked upon apprehensively by the teacher. The teacher will not be replaced, but his primary function will be concerned with the diagnosis of individual learning problems, supplying guidance and leading class discussions.

TEAM TEACHING

Much has been said about team teaching and, unfortunately, there is much confusion and a certain mystery about what true team teaching really is. Actually, there is no single approach to team teaching. Yet, most educators would agree that it is a pliable program in which a group of teachers cooperatively plan and share their ideas. They evolve specific instructional objectives and lessons and are constantly reviewing and evaluating their successes and failures.

The number of people appearing on the team will vary, depending on staffing and facilities in the school where the team teaching program is in effect. In many programs there is generally a team leader, two or more regular classroom teachers, and perhaps specialists assisted by teaching interns and teachers' aides. Team teaching should not do away with the self-contained classroom, since this traditional form of grouping includes certain advantages for individual and independent study.

A sound team teaching program brings together teachers' complementary talents, skills and strengths, for the fulfillment of each team's role. Team teaching also provides the machinery for shifting of instructional roles, for under this program, the individual teacher can take advantage of his abilities and mastery of certain subject areas or may be intrigued with its application to the core curriculum program. Actual team teaching should capitalize on the individual differences of people on the team.

Any team teaching program, to be successful, must be tailored to fit the school system in which it is to function. One form of team teaching may work very well in one community, and in another system it might be unworkable. There are some school systems that boast they have team teaching, but in actuality, are just departmentalized or have two teachers in a self-contained classroom.

A good team teaching program will rely in large measure on audio-visual materials. For example, motion pictures and the overhead projector are specifically suited to large class instruction. Audio disc recordings, tapes and filmstrips are very helpful in small group and individual instruction.

NON-GRADED SCHOOL

The elementary school in the past ten years has become the scene of a number of experiments which are serving to alter the structure and patterns of school organization. Team teaching is only one of these innovational changes. There are other experimental reforms, such as a multi-age grouping, multi-tracking and non-grading programs.

Interest in the non-graded approach to school organization has been intensified where educators are seeking a more flexible teaching program than seems possible under the traditional graded program still in effect in most American schools. A substantial number of educators are convinced that only the non-graded school approach can meet the demands and complexities of our modern automated world.

In the purely non-graded school, arbitrary grade level designations are removed along with unrealistic grade expectation. The main argument for non-gradedness is that in removing grade level plateaus, children are free to progress at their own rates of speed without the stigma or fear of failure. Advocates of non-graded structure maintain that the curriculum is geared to meet the needs of the pupils, and they believe that non-gradedness, since it removes tensions over promotion, results in an atmosphere of better mental health. Supporters of non-graded structure also feel that pupils develop a greater self-reliance due in part to the extensive and intelligent utilization of self-instructed materials.

It is quite obvious from an analysis of literature, surveys and research of non-graded programs, that there will be heavy reliance on the implements of audio-visual instruction. Certainly, the introductions of programmed learning materials, listening carrels, Dial Access and computer-assisted instruction are even more compatible, and are of undeniable value to the ungraded school program.

HOW TO KEEP PACE WITH CURRENT AUDIO-VISUAL TRENDS AND CURRICULUM CHANGES

The best way for teachers to keep abreast of developments in the audio-visual field is to be an avid reader. Frequent perusal of educational literature, namely, professional magazines such as *The Instructor, Grade Teacher, Today's Education, Audiovisual Instruction,* and *Educational Screen AV Guide,* will enable the classroom teacher to stay well informed on the newest audio-visual equipment and techniques of media education, and make him aware of any significant experimentation. Professional magazines, because they are published on a monthly basis, are better able to keep the reader up-to-date with changes in audio-visual technology and methodology.

There are, of course, many fine audio-visual books that survey the entire audio-visual field in depth, but even the authors of these texts will admit that their works should be supplemented by reading current literature.

It is also a good idea to get on the mailing list of key audio-visual manufacturers who will be only too happy to send you literature descriptive of their new products. *Educational Screen AV Guide* publishes every August a special issue entitled "The Annual Bluebook of Audio-Visual Materials," which is a current and comprehensive listing of filmstrips, films, slide sets and recordings that have been recently produced and released. The *Educational Media Index* (14 volumes), published by McGraw-Hill, is perhaps the best source of information for most audio-visual materials produced in the past few years. It is an indexed inventory of non-printed educational materials such as films, filmstrips, flat pictures, models, disc recordings, audio tapes, programmed instruction, video tapes, slides and transparencies. Each volume contains materials for subject and instructional areas. Annual supplements are meeting the problem of obsolescence.

Most teachers will find worthwhile, attendance at district and state conferences where audio-visual distributors and exhibits can be viewed. The most comprehensive and profitable convention, from the viewpoint of the teacher and administrator, is the DAVI (Department of Audio-visual Instruction—NEA) Convention, held annually.

Many school districts and colleges offer in-service courses and workshop seminars taught by competently trained personnel. These are most worthwhile in removing the veil of mystery and unawareness that sometimes surrounds the wonderful world of audio-visual aids.

SUMMARY

In the foreseeable future, programmed learning, Dial Access, language laboratories and computer-assisted instruction will be terms as common-place as were text and chalkboard in the past. Sometimes it is hard to speculate about tomorrow's world of audio-visuals, but obviously, it will be a fascinating place in which to teach and learn.

DIRECTORY OF
AUDIO-VISUAL
MANUFACTURERS

American Optical Co. (Instrument Division), Eggert and Sugar Roads, Buffalo, N.Y. 14215—Overhead, opaque and slide projectors.

Ampex Corporation, Consumer and Educational Products Division, 2201 Lunt, Elk Grove Village, Ill. 60007—Random access audio information retrieval system.

Association Instructional Materials, 600 Madison Ave., New York, N.Y. 10022 —Film materials.

Audiotronics Corporation, 7428 Bellaire Ave., North Hollywood, Calif. 91605 —Classroom record and transcription players, radios, tape recorders, listening systems, AV accessories.

Bell and Howell Audio-Visual Products Division, 7100 McCormick Rd., Chicago, Ill. 60645—16mm automatic threading projectors, automatic filmstrip projectors, language masters.

The Charles Beseler Company, 219 S. 18th St., East Orange, N.J. 07018—Overhead and opaque projection equipment.

Stanley Bowmar Co., Inc., 4 Broadway, Valhalla, N.Y. 10595—Filmstrips and records covering most curriculum areas.

Bowmar Records, Inc., 622 Rodier Drive, Glendale, Calif. 91201—Educational recordings, posters.

Buhl Projector Co., Inc., 1776 New Highway, Farmingdale, N.Y. 11735—Overhead projectors, accessories, and supplies.

Caedmon Records, Inc., 505 Eighth Ave., New York, N.Y. 10018—Records and prerecorded tapes.

Contemporary Films, 330 West 42nd St., New York, N.Y. 10036—Motion pictures.

Coronet Instructional Films, 65 East South Water St., Chicago, Ill. 60601— 16mm sound educational motion pictures, Coronet Learning Programs.

Denoyer-Geppert Company, 5235 Ravenswood Ave., Chicago, Ill. 60640— Maps, globes, charts, models, microscopes, transparencies, etc.

DuKane Corp., St. Charles, Ill. 60174—Filmstrip projectors and sound filmstrip projectors.

Eastman Kodak Company, 343 State St., Rochester, N.Y. 14650—Audiovisual equipment.

Educational Activities, Inc., 1937 Grand Ave., Baldwin, N.Y. 11510—Records.

Educational Developmental Laboratories, 284 E. Pulaski Rd., Huntington, N.Y. 11744—Developmental reading equipment and materials.

Encyclopaedia Britannica Educational Corp., 425 North Michigan Ave., Chicago, Ill. 60611—16mm educational films, filmstrips, 8mm study prints, overhead transparencies.

Enrichment Teaching Materials, 246 Fifth Ave., New York, N.Y. 10001— Educational records and filmstrips.

Eye Gate House, Inc., 146-01 Archer Ave., Jamaica, N.Y. 11435—Filmstrips and charts.

Fairchild Camera and Instrument Corp., 221 Fairchild Ave., Plainview, N.Y. 11803—8mm read-screen projection equipment.

Folkways/Scholastic Records, 50 West 44th St., New York, N.Y. 10036—Records.

GAF Corporation (General Aniline and Film Corp.), 140 W. 51 St., New York, N.Y. 10020—Prepared transparencies, overhead projector.

Hammond, Incorporated, 515 Valley St., Maplewood, New Jersey 07040— Transparencies, maps (wall atlases), map-record sets.

Imperial International Learning, 247 West Court St., Kankakee, Illinois 60901—Preprogrammed tapes.

Instructional Aids, Inc., Box 293, Owatonna, Minn. 55056—Modern aids and curriculum color prints.

The Instructo Corporation, Paoli, Pa. 19301—Instructo teaching transparencies for elementary-junior high grades, flannel board sets.

The Jam Handy Organization, 2821 East Grand Blvd., Detroit, Michigan 48211—Filmstrips, recordings, 8mm and 16mm motion pictures.

The Kalart Company, Hultenius St., Plainville, Conn. 06062—Kalart/Victor audiovisual products, Kalart Tele-Beam.

Keystone View Co., Meadville, Pa. 16335—Teaching machines, reading training equipment, vision screening equipment.

McGraw-Hill Book Co., Text-Film Division, 330 West 42nd St., New York, N.Y. 10036—Educational audiovisual materials.

Charles Mayer Studios, Inc., 776 Commins St., Akron, Ohio 44307—Hook N' Loop, flannel, Magnetic boards, easels.

MLA-Modern Learning Aids, Div. of Modern Talking Picture Service, Inc., 1212 Avenue of the Americas, New York, N.Y. 10036—16mm films.

Moody Institute of Science (Educational Film Div.), Santa Monica Blvd., W. Los Angeles, Calif. 11428—Science films.

Newcomb Audio Products Co., 12881 Bradley Ave., Sylmar, Calif. 91342— Classroom phonographs, radios, recorders, transcription players, headphone listening centers, P.A. systems.

A. J. Nystrom and Co., 3333 Elston Ave., Chicago, Ill. 60618—Maps, globes, charts, models.

Popular Science Publishing Co., Audio-Visual Div., 355 Lexington Ave., New York, N.Y. 10017—Filmstrips.

RCA Instructional Electronics, Building 15-5, Camden, N.J. 08102—16mm projectors, television, language labs.

RCA Record Division, 155 E. 24th St., New York, N.Y. 10010—Children's records.

Rheem Califone, 5922 Bowcroft St., Los Angeles, Calif. 90016—Record players, tape recorders, language laboratories, sound systems, Dial Access Retrieval Systems.

Sandak, Inc., 4 East 48th St., New York, N.Y. 10017—Color slides.

Seal, Inc., 251 Roosevelt Dr., Derby, Conn. 06418—Seal dry mounting/laminating presses, Seal-Lamin laminating film.

Sing 'N Do Records, 214 Godwin Ave., Midland, N.J.—Activities records.

Society for Visual Education, Inc. (A Subsidiary of General Precision Equipment Corp.), 1343 Diversey Pkwy., Chicago, Ill. 60614.

Sony Corporation of America, VTR Division, 47-47 Van Dam St., Long Island City, N.Y. 11101—Videotape recorders, television monitors, television cameras.

Standard Projector and Equipment Co., Inc., 1911 Pickwick Ave., Glenview, Ill., 60025—Filmstrip projectors, combination filmstrip and slide projectors, filmstrip viewers, sound-slidefilm projectors, record players.

Tapes Unlimited, 13113 Puritan Ave., Detroit, Mich. 48227—Prerecorded tapes.

Technicolor, Inc., Commercial and Ed. Div., 1300 Frawley Dr., Costa Mesa, Calif. 92627—Technicolor cartridge-loading instant movie projector.

Tecnifax/Visucom, 20 First Ave., Chicopee, Mass. 01020—Transparencies and related instructional materials.

3M Co., Wollensak Division, 2501 Hudson Rd., St. Paul, Minn. 55101—Wollensak tape recorders and "Scotch" brand magnetic recording tape.

3M Visual Products Div., 2501 Hudson Rd., St. Paul, Minn. 55101—Overhead projectors, transparency maker-copiers, film, copy paper, and accessories.

Viewlex, Inc., One Broadway Ave., Holbrook, N.Y. 11741—Slide and Filmstrip projectors, 8mm and 16mm motionpicture equipment, and transparency copy machines.

V-M Corp., 305 Territorial Rd., Benton Harbor, Mich. 49022—Tape recorders and school phonographs.

Ward's, P.O. Box 1712, Rochester, N.Y. 14603—Study prints.

Webster Electric Co., 1900 Clark St., Racine, Wis. 53403—Language laboratories, stenographic laboratories, sound 7 communications.

Weston Woods, Inc., Weston, Conn. 06880—Silent and sound filmstrips, motion pictures and recordings.

H. Wilson Corp., 555 W. 166 St., South Holland, Ill. 60473—Projector, mobile AV, and ETV tables, TV wall and ceiling mounts, mobile read-projection units.

BIBLIOGRAPHY

Brown, James W., Richard B. Lewis and Fred F. Harcleroad, *A-V Instruction: Materials and Methods*. New York: McGraw-Hill, 1964.

Cross, A. J. and Irene F. Cypher, *Audio-Visual Education*. New York: Crowell, 1961.

Educational Media Index. New York: McGraw-Hill, 1964.

Freedman, Florence, B. and Esther L. Berg, *Classroom Teacher's Guide to Audio-Visual Material*. Philadelphia: Chilton, 1961.

Kemp, Jerrold E., *Planning and Producing Audiovisual Materials*. San Francisco: Chandler, 1963.

Miner, Ed, *Simplified Techniques for Preparing Visual Instruction Materials*. New York: McGraw-Hill, 1962.

Morlan, John E., *Preparation of Inexpensive Teaching Materials*. San Francisco: Chandler, 1963.

Pula, Fred John, *Application and Operation of Audiovisual Equipment in Education*. New York: John Wiley, 1968.

Scuorzo, Herbert E., *The Practical Audio-Visual Handbook for Teachers*. West Nyack, New York: Parker, 1967.

Thomas, R. Murray and Sherwin G. Swartout, *Integrated Teaching Materials*. New York: Longmans, 1960.

Wittich, Walter Arne and Charles Francis Schuller, *Audio-Visual Materials: Their Nature and Use*. New York: Harper, 1962.

KEY
EDUCATIONAL
PERIODICALS

Audiovisual Instruction   Dept. of Audiovisual Instruction of National Educators Association, 1201 16 St., N.W. Washington, D.C. 20036.

Educational Screen Audiovisual and AV Guide   434 South Wabash, Chicago, Illinois 60605.

Grade Teacher   Teachers Publishing Corp., 23 Leroy Avenue, Darien, Conn. 06820.

Scholastic Teacher   (Elementary Edition) Scholastic Magazine, Inc., 50 West 44th Street, New York, N.Y. 10036.

The Instructor   (Instructor Publications Inc., Subsidiary) Harcourt, Brace & World, Inc., Instructor Park, Dansville, N.Y. 11437.

Today's Education   (Journal of National Education Association) National Education Association, 1201 16 St., N.W. Washington, D.C. 20036.

INDEX

the overhead projector to illustrate the concept of sets . . . relate geometric shapes to their names . . . show linear and angular measurement . . . put meaning into basic arithmetic operations . . . and demonstrate key mathematical rules. How to use models and relia for teaching measurement, chart construction and use.

SCIENCE: How to use the tape recorder for a multitude of science research activities, to capture scientific radio or TV programs, and to teach characteristics of the sounds of nature and machines. How to use the opaque and overhead projectors to perform demonstrations such as chemical changes or reactions . . . examine and identify rocks, shells, insects, animals, or leaves . . . teach optics and vision principles . . . demonstrate such concepts as magnetism, polarized light, sound wave patterns, surface tension, and the inclined plane.

In addition, you'll discover scores of methods, activities and ideas for improving learning through the optimum use of audio-visual aids in:

- **Spelling**
- **Writing**
- **Oral Expression**
- **Music**
- **Art**
- **Social Studies**
- **Physical Education**
- **Library Science**

Whenever you need them, you can instantly find exactly the audio-visual aids you want for your particular grade and subject. Thus you'll avoid the time-consuming task of hunting through the book to find, for instance, a good suggestion for tomorrow's reading lesson, or the following day's lesson in social studies.

This new volume covers virtually every aspect of the successful audio-visual aids program . . . with everything worked out for you in lucid, step-by-step detail . . . everything you need to put your present program on an outstandingly increased level of effectiveness.